THE PLYNLIMON & HAFAN TRAMWAY

A brief description of the

Plynlimon and Hafan Narrow Guage

2 ft. 3in. Tramline,

and the district it traverses

and will serve.

HARVEY, TYPO.

Cover of 1896 pamphlet

THE PLYNLIMON & HAFAN TRAMWAY

BY

E. A. WADE

TWELVEHEADS PRESS

TRURO 1997

CONTENTS

UNITS

The units used throughout this book are those current at the time of the Plynlimon & Hafan Tramway. They may be converted as follows:

Length:	1 foot = 12 inches = 0.3048 metres 1 yard = 3 feet = 36 inches = 0.9144 metres 1 mile = 80 chains = 1,760 yards = 1.609 kilometres
Weight:	1 ton = 20 cwt 1 cwt = 112 pounds (lb)
Money:	£1 = 20 shillings = 100p 1 shilling (s) = 12 pence (d)

TWELVEHEADS PRESS

First published 1976 by Gemini Publishing Co.
This edition published 1997 by Twelveheads Press, Chy Mengleth, Twelveheads, Truro, Cornwall TR4 8SN.
ISBN 0 906294 38 X
British Library Cataloguing-in-Publication Data.
A cataogue record for this book is available from the British Library.

Designed by Alan Kittridge. Printed by The Amadeus Press Ltd., Huddersfield.

PREFACE
TO THE SECOND EDITION

When this book first appeared, some twenty years ago, it was published privately by the author and sold, in the main, by mail order. Only one thousand copies were printed and it had sold out within eighteen months; since when it has become, despite a rather poor binding, something of a collector's item. As the one hundredth anniversary of the opening of the Plynlimon and Hafan Tramway will occur in 1997, the author has been persuaded by the publisher of his second book (*The Redlake Tramway and China Clay Works*, 1982) to revise the manuscript of the first for a second edition.

Very little new information has come to light since the first edition and the present book is, essentially, a reprint of the former, in a different format, with the addition of some illustrations and information and the correction of a few factual and grammatical errors.

Various articles have been published, since the first edition, which touch on items of the tramway's rolling stock and these have been listed in an extended bibliography. One article, by Rodney Weaver, dealt extensively with the design of the tramway's unusual first steam locomotive, *Victoria*, and this has been reprinted, along with the present author's responses thereto, in an appendix. The appendix in the first edition dealing with 'local railway relics' has been substantially modified in the light of research by Robert Nicholls which has disproved certain suppositions.

Should any reader possess information or material relating to the Plynlimon and Hafan Tramway, the company and individuals who ran it or the mines and quarry which it served, the author would be most pleased to hear from them.

E.A.Wade 1997...for Elaine

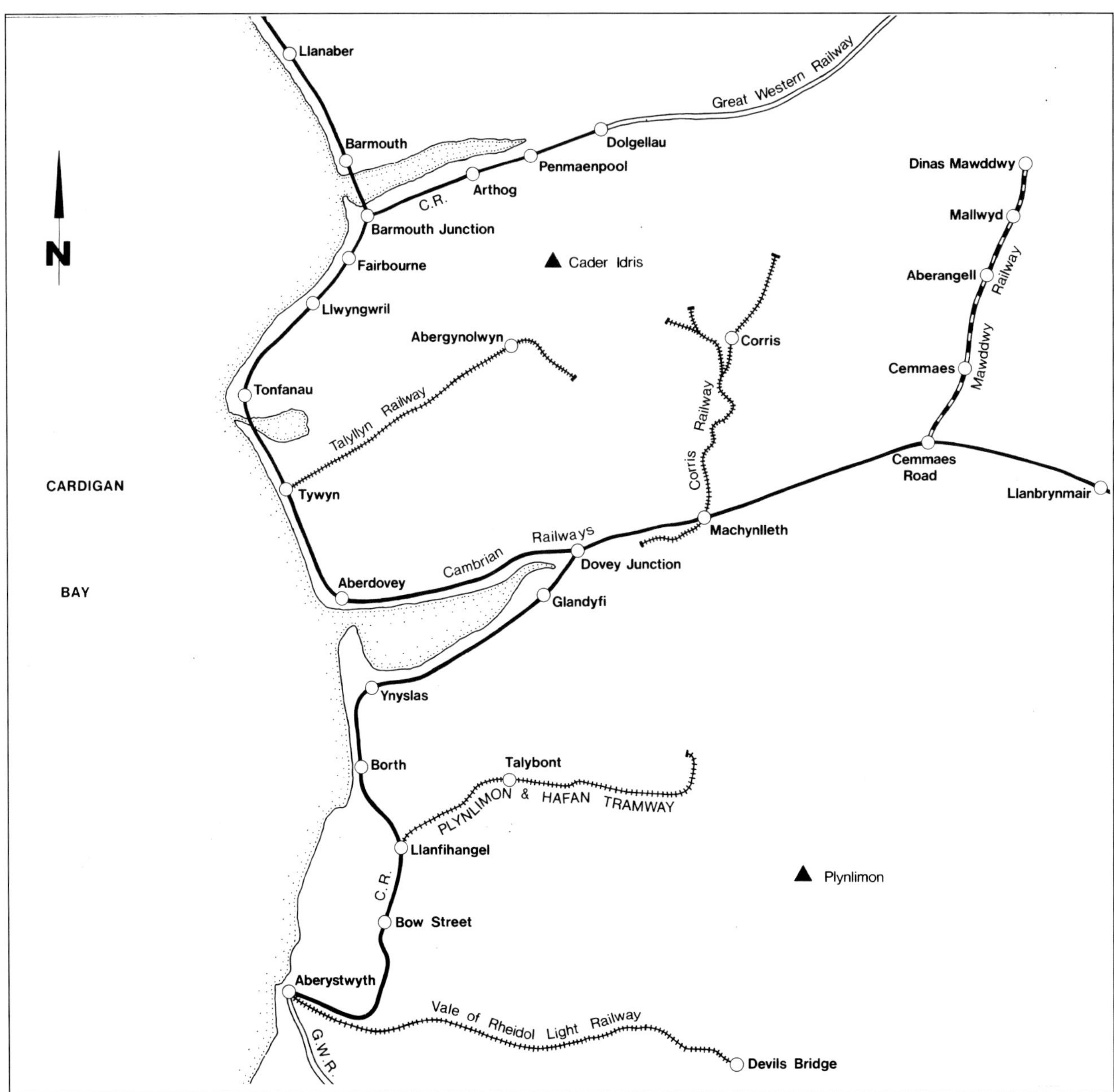

Railways in the Machynlleth area

INTRODUCTION

Wales is a land of contrasts. The south has long been a great industrial centre and north Wales has flourished for many years, under the patronage of tourists besides being, in the nineteenth and early twentieth centuries, the home of the world's largest slate industry.

Mid Wales by comparison, is to this day a bleak though beautiful, unpopulated region despite the impetus given by the establishment of the University of Wales at Aberystwyth. It is this remoteness which has made the area the stronghold of the Welsh language and which is partly responsible for making the Plynlimon and Hafan Tramway (otherwise known as the Hafan Railway or the Hafan Tram) the most obscure of the passenger carrying Welsh narrow gauge railways; the other major factor being its extremely brief existence. The tramway's history revolves around a financier from Lancashire, a Welsh mining engineer and the local landowner of the ancient and noble Pryse family, which represented Cardiganshire in Parliament from Tudor times until the twentieth century. It came into being as an outlet for various small scale mining and quarrying ventures in the Plynlimon foothills and ceased to exist when these ventures brought their promoter near to bankruptcy. Its life, though short, was colourful.

A bibliography appears at the end of this volume but three works must be mentioned at the outset as they are referred to in the following pages. The first documentation of the tramway appeared in J. I. C. Boyd's *Narrow Gauge Railways in Mid-Wales* which was first published in 1952 (Second Edition 1970) and was followed, in 1955, by Lewis Cozens' booklet *The Plynlimon and Hafan Tramway*, which heretofore constituted the most detailed account of the line. The third work is W. J. K. Davies' booklet *The Vale of Rheidol Light Railway* (1970) which contains information relating to certain items of rolling stock, formerly running on the Plynlimon line. Further research has occupied most of my spare time for two years, in which time I have walked many miles, written countless letters and imposed on the time and good nature of many people. The result you now have before you and it is hoped that you will consider it worth the effort.

E. A. Wade 1976

CHAPTER ONE

HEADING FOR THE HILLS

Travellers on the mainline railway from Machynlleth, south to Aberystwyth, will notice that, after passing through Borth station, the line turns away from the coast. In company with a minor road, it follows the course of a river between the hills. It twice passes over and then plunges beneath this road and emerges from its cutting to pass through an ungated crossing. Beyond where the gates once were lies Llandre station, some 5 miles 72 chains short of Aberystwyth and 153 feet above sea level, but the station building has now been converted to a private dwelling. The trains have not stopped here since 1965 and will probably never do so again, so let us go back to the closing years of the last century and re-examine the scene. In those days the station possessed two sidings and was under the ownership of the Cambrian Railways. The sign boards read 'Llanfihangel' serving, as it did, the parish of Llanfihangel Geneu'r-glyn (the station was renamed about 1916). Passing through the level crossing, to the north of the station, an exchange siding was constructed by the Cambrian in 1897 of some 835 feet in length (it was lifted in 1911). From this siding ran a 2 feet 3 inch gauge tramway and it is with that tramway that this history is concerned.

At the south end of the exchange siding, in the corner formed with the road, was said to have stood a stonecutting shed but this, like the siding itself, has been lost following a widening of the road and the rebuilding of the main line station. Beyond the siding the tramway had a run round loop, which also did service as a passenger station and is said to have been graced with a small wooden ticket office. The single track then curved away to the north-east, through an area since planted with conifers by the council, and crossed the Borth road on the level. The conifers now (1996) have a new house in their midst, for which the level of the ground has been considerably raised, and to the east of the Borth road the gardens of a new

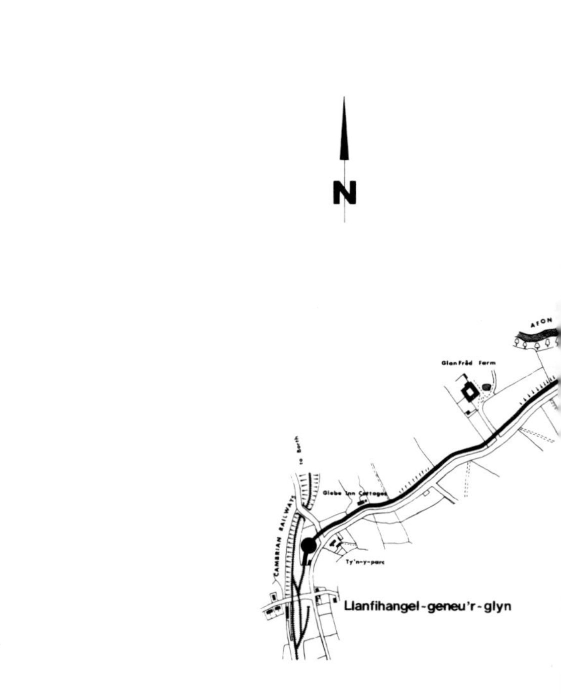

Llanfihangel – Talybont – Pontbren-geifr

housing estate cover the route. Then, clinging to the northern side of the road to Talybont, the track passed in front of Glebe Inn Cottages (22 chains). These cottages still exist but beyond them the course of the line is now lost owing to relatively new housing developments. The line then ran in a shallow cutting, from which it emerged to cross the lane to Glanfraed Farm (57 chains), now shared with the entrance to the Riverside Park caravan and campsite, and continued on a low embankment, separated from the road by a hedge, with a fine view of the valley ahead. After passing through a cutting, up to ten feet deep in one place, over which was erected a bridge for the passage of farm livestock and carts (1 mile 22 chains) the tramway parted company with the road. The cuttings and embankments along this stretch of the route are gradually being filled and levelled by the farmer and all trace will eventually be lost. It cut across the fields on an embankment to the corner of Coed-y-cwm where, lost in the edge of the wood, there still stands a magnificent bridge and stone embankment. It was built as a cattle creep and for the haulage of timber from the wood on the insistence of Mr James Thomas Morgan who owned nearby Maesnewydd Farm. The farm has been occupied by the Morgan family for more than 300 years and

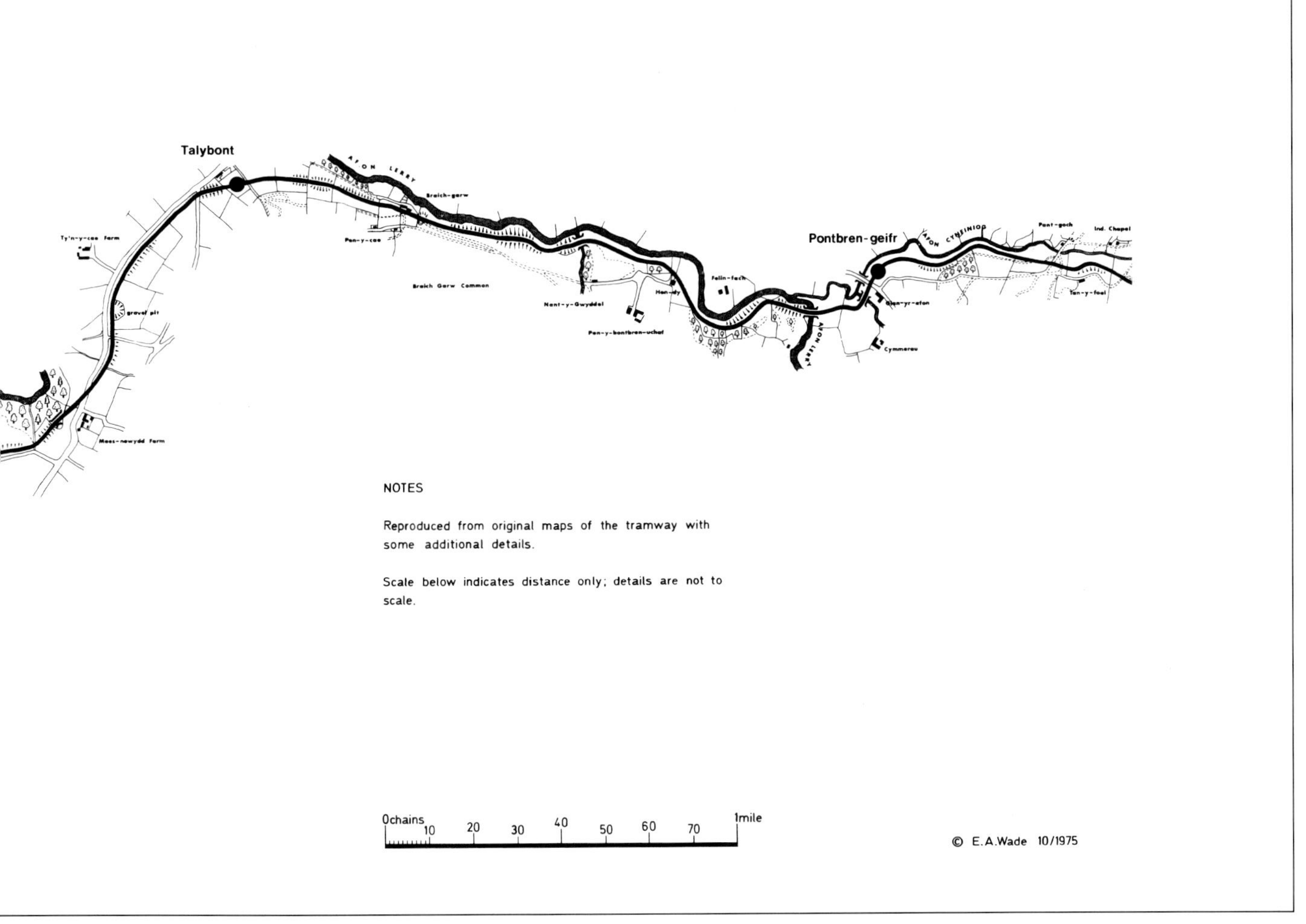

now the grandson of J. T. Morgan is in possession. The tramway then cut back across the fields to cross the main Aberystwyth to Talybont road on the level at an acute angle (1 mile 49 chains). It followed the road, behind the hedge, on the south-east side for some distance, climbing steadily with a series of embankments (up to some 12 feet high at one point) and cuttings. Being the main Aberystwyth to Machynlleth road, it has been considerably improved over the years and bears little relationship to the road which existed at the time of the tramway. Traces of the old winding road can still be discerned in a cutting on the east side of the modern road and the cuttings and embankments of the tramway will be found beyond the hedge, along the edge of the fields to the east of the old road. The gradient of the modern road is much closer to that of the tramway than it is to the old road. At the site of the old mile post (seven miles by road from Aberystwyth) both road and rail were 225 feet above sea level but from this point the road drops very steeply into Talybont and, after crossing a lane, the tramway was forced to take another route, across country.

Running around the hill on an embankment, the line pulled into Pen-y-Rhiw (Top of the Hill) station (2 miles 21 chains) high on the hill above Talybont. The station was reached by a footpath, which no longer exists, and consisted of an engine shed with inspection pit and water tower, run round loop and the wooden Company's Office, which ended its days as a hen

The bridge in the corner of Coed-y-cwm.
NATIONAL MONUMENTS RECORD FOR WALES

coop on Glanfraed Farm. The original plans of the line show a station building also but it does not appear on any photographs and it is doubtful if it was ever built.The layout of the station on its ledge was to be seen until early 1974, when the ground was turned over. The track continued around the hill and through a shallow cutting, now waterlogged (2½ miles), and on to a long embankment which took it behind Braich-garw cottage, where a concrete stable block has been erected on the course of the track. Emerging on the other side, the tramway crosses a track to Pen-y-bontbren-uchaf Farm on the level and the Afon Leri (formerly anglicised as the River Lerry) can now be seen a few yards below, to the north. At the point where the tramway crosses the track there is a small quarry on the southern side, its spoil tip being on the north. A public seat graced the flat top of the spoil heap for some years, giving a good view up the valley. A gate has recently (1996) been erected across the trackbed at this point to prevent cars from driving along it (which is no doubt sensible but has deprived the author of one of his favourite camp sites slightly further along the line). The route continues on a high embankment, built with stone from the Braich-garw quarry, straight across the common land with the level of the river rising to meet it. And meet they do, for the trackbed delves into a rock cutting which curves slightly to the south and, on emerging, falls into the river (3½ miles). This cutting, it appears, was formerly much longer, carrying the tramway through the narrowing valley below the 900 feet Braich Garw. However, being on a bend in the river,

Washday in Talybont, with 1497 raising steam in the rather untidy station. Access was by the footpath, under the tree, in the centre foreground. The White Lion and the Black Lion line the rear of the village square. The view is to the north and the debis in the station may indicate the unfinished state of the works.
NATIONAL LIBRARY OF WALES

the formation has been and continues to be steadily washed away.

The trackbed reappears just before crossing the Nant-y-Gwyddil (3 miles 27 chains) on a bridge of which only the small abutments remain. It continues, clinging to the south bank of the Leri, below Pen-y-bontbren-uchaf Farm and the old Lerry Valley Mine. There is a small stonebuilt store on the southern side followed by a beautifully constructed stone slab retaining wall. The southern bank then gives way to fields, alongside which the track is carried on a low embankment separated from the river by trees. The Afon Leri now turns sharply to the south and the abutments of the bridge which carried the tramway across are still to be seen (4 miles 5 chains). The track follows the valley of the Afon Cyneiniog *en route* for Pontbren-geifr and, on the way, it crosses the Afon Cwmere which flows into the Cyneiniog from the south. The line emerges at Pontbren-geifr next to the river and at the end of the garden adjoining the blacksmith's cottage. The wooden smithy, next to the cottage, still stood in 1976 though out of use for some years, but has now disappeared while the cottage has been 'gentrified', losing all of its charm in the process. Crossing the road on the level, immediately south of the river bridge, the tramway passed into a field where there was situated a trailing siding (4 miles 26 chains). This 'station' marked the normal limit of the passenger service.

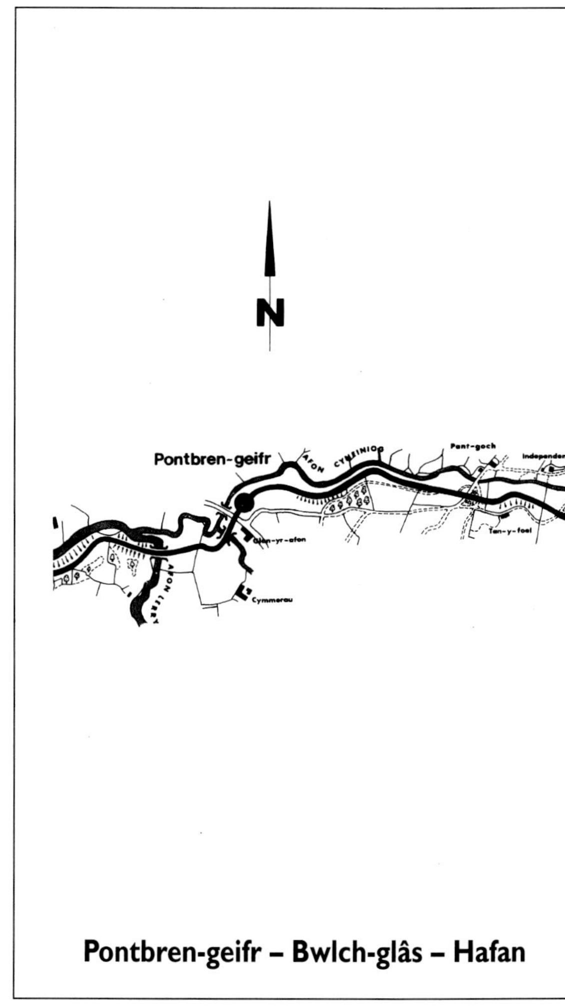

Pontbren-geifr – Bwlch-glâs – Hafan

CHAPTER TWO

ABOVE THE TREE LINE

The line continues from Pontbren-geifr by the side of the Afon Cyneiniog with a series of cuttings and embankments until it reaches the lane to Ty-nant Farm (4 miles 75 chains). It crosses the lane, again on the level, and plunges into a short but very deep rock cutting. From this point the tramway steadily climbs the hillside, drawing away from the Cyneiniog, and crosses over the mountain road at a sharp angle before reaching a small underbridge of which the abutments remain ($5^1/_2$ miles). Within a quarter of a mile it passes into a wood above Dolgarn-wen Farm where a dozen or so sleepers are still to be seen; all very rotten now and many strewn about haphazardly. Some still contain their original bolts and dog spikes. From this point the last 62 chains of track were finally removed in about 1926.

Leaving the wood, the tramway

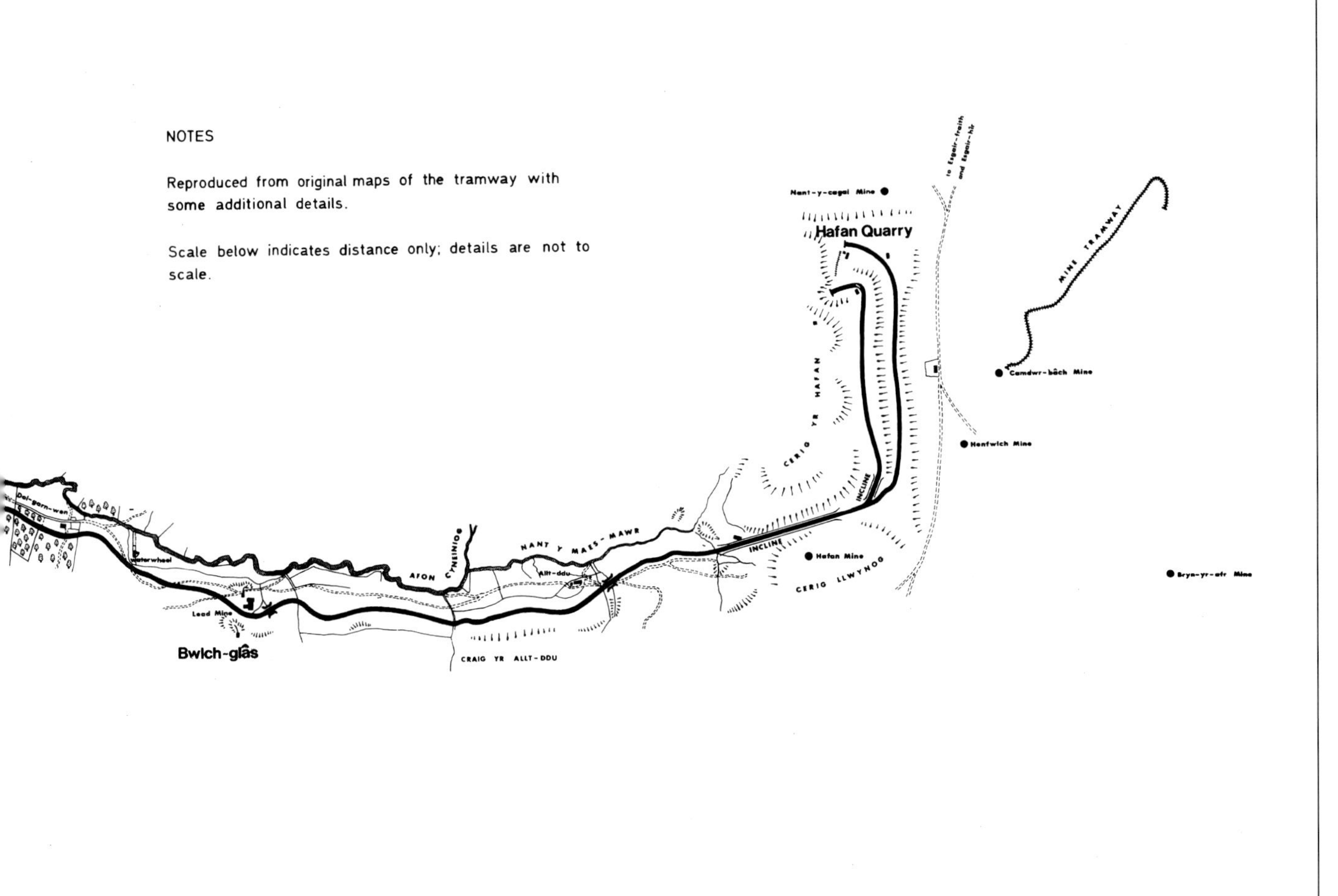

Bwlch-glâs lead mine in the early 1920s. The tramway ran just behind the tower and on the ledge in the left background. The run of mill buildings down the hillside, the foundations of which may still be traced on site, indicate how gravity was utilised in the processing of ore.
NATIONAL LIBRARY OF WALES

runs beneath the slopes of the 1,040 feet Moel Golomen to reach the Bwlch-glâs Lead Mine where its route, between the main buildings, is now partly covered by spoil tips. The Bwlch-glâs Mine was worked in 1882, 1887, 1889, 1909-11, 1913-16 and then intermittently until 1923. The last company to work it was the Scottish Cardigan Lead Mining Co. (see photograph) in 1920-23. A little work was done in 1934 but this was in the nature of a clearing up operation. The remains of some Kerr Stuart wagons were found on the spoil tip in the 1960s, probably dating from the 1913-16 working period. During its life it produced a total of 1,240 tons of lead ore, 6,361 ounces of silver and an official output of 99 tons of zinc. However, the figure for zinc is debatable as it was frequently stockpiled to be sold when the price was right (it was often used as ballast for ships and in road construction). The total output was probably in excess of 1,000 tons. It seems strange that the mine should not have been worked during the life of the tramway, as the company that owned the line also owned the mine and as the route was obviously designed with this in mind. If it had done the tramway would undoubtedly have had a somewhat longer existence. Just beyond the mine are the abutments of another small underbridge, followed by the remains of yet more sleepers, now almost hidden under the grass. The gradient becomes more severe as the track enters a short rock cutting (the eastern limit of the 1926 track lifting) and the route, which was blocked in 1976 by trees and undergrowth in a new Forestry Commission plantation, is passable once more in 1996. Cut into the side of the hill it provides a pleasant path through the spruce forest; the large outcrops of rock, through which the tramway had to be cut, now hung with moss and lichen. Two lengths of flat bottomed rail are discernable where they have been used to strengthen a partially collapsed culvert at the side of the trackbed. We are now 750 feet above sea level and, but for the Forestry Commission, above the tree line. The Cyneiniog is 600 feet away to the north and far below us.

When the tramway emerges from the plantation, opposite Cyneiniog Farm, it has risen another 75 feet. Perched on a stone embankment on the mountainside, it continues below the Allt-ddu escarpment and above the last dwelling in the valley, which bears the same name (now just a ruin). The line crosses a rushing mountain stream on a high bridge (again only the abutments remain) and we are now 900 feet above the sea. The tramway then climbs a further 57 feet to reach the end of the main line at the foot of the Hafan Incline (7 miles 26 chains). The trackbed, at this point, has been steadily washed away by a stream. Formerly there were two exchange sidings, one to each side of the track (the first to the right of the main line and the second to the left) followed by a run round loop. The incline was double tracked with a winding drum at the top and empty wagons were pulled up on a rope by the weight of the loaded ones going down. The incline raised the line by 400 feet through a slope of about 21 degrees (1 in 2.6). Near the foot of the incline, on the north side, are the remains of the wheel pit of an old overshot waterwheel which supplied power to the Hafan Mine, before the time of the tramway, and the leat which brought the water from a nearby stream is still discernable. The adit to the mine is

TALYBONT and the carriage on a special excursion at the foot of the incline. They are standing at the start of the exchange sidings. Note the remains of the Hafan Mine water wheel pit to the left of the incline. The undulating condition of the incline track may be the result of either poor or unfinished construction. NATIONAL LIBRARY OF WALES

about half way up on the south side and some old drainage outlets are to be seen near the foot. The Hafan Mine has been in existence since 1698 and was worked in conjunction with the Henfwlch Mine, which lies in the valley beyond the incline. A chimney and a gable wall are all that remain of the latter. Nobody knows what the total output of the Hafan Mine was, as records have only been compulsory since 1854. Between 1854 and 1864, when the mine was closed, it was operative for only six years. During this time it produced 623 tons of lead ore, 4 tons of zinc and 25 tons of copper ore.

From the top of the incline, 1,360 feet above sea level, one is rewarded for the climb with a fine view back down the valley to the west, and the course of the tramway may be quite easily discerned. The trackbed, at this point, has been obliterated by a now deserted quarry which was opened by McAlpines when they built the dam for the nearby Nant-y-môch Reservoir, between 1956 and 1961. The remains of the winding drum (to the north side of the line) were also destroyed during this operation, as were various exchange sidings. Beyond the quarry, the track may be relocated just before a second incline branches off to the north. This upper incline is far shorter than the main incline and was almost certainly single tracked. It is not known what method was used for raising and lowering the wagons on it. The two extensions run virtually parallel all the way to the quarry but, until they reach it, it is the lower line which proves the most interesting, Shortly after separating both lines turn sharply to the north (the lower line has been partly cut away) and the lower plunges into another conifer plantation. From this point one is afforded another excellent view, across the new reservoir to the slopes of Plynlimon, 3½ miles east-south-east and 2,468 feet above sea level. The trackbed had been used as a 'ride' to assist in the maintenance of the plantation and was still plainly visible twenty years ago but young trees have grown up to make it impassable. No doubt it will be clear once more by 2016! Several trial workings could be seen to the west of this lower line with small spoil tips to the east. Eventually, both lines turn westwards and enter the

The upper incline with an indication of the line of the upper and lower extensions. E. A. WADE

This rare photograph is the only one known to the author taken in Hafan Quarry, and may not have been taken during the short lifetime of the tramway. The five men are producing paving sets by the time honoured method of brute force. At the rear one man holds a chisel or drill while the other strikes it with a hammer. The stone does appear to break very squarely but there is a large amount of waste rock on the left.
NATIONAL LIBRARY OF WALES

two main levels of the Hafan Quarry (a small, third level is apparent higher up the hill). Both lines are more or less level for their entire length. Judging by the tightness of the curve where the upper track enters the upper level, it seems likely that the locomotive ran on the lower track. However, the upper level is a far more extensive working; the remains of sidings, on top of five spoil tips, and various buildings may be seen. The working is sometimes known as the 'Setts Quarry' as paving setts were one of its main products. Cozens states that the quarry stone is granite and Boyd that it is limestone. In fact it is 'greywacke', a coarse textured sandstone.

Little is known of the layout inside the quarry, although the 1906 OS map shows a length of tramway connecting the two levels. Presumably there was also some form of run round loop for the locomotive.

The output of stone from the Hafan Quarry in the year 25 June 1897 to 25 June 1898 (the only period for which records exist) amounts to 1,690 tons 4 cwt and the clients included Birmingham Corporation, the Mid Wales Mining Co, the Warrington Slate Co Ld, Cardigan County Council, the Corporation of Aberystwyth, Mr P. P. Pryse and various local contractors.

CHAPTER THREE

CONCEPTION

1890–1892

The difficulties inherent in exploiting the natural resources of remote areas, without the advantage of suitable transport and communication systems, are illustrated by the record of failure of companies attempting to extract ore from the Leri valley. On 12 April 1866 the Plynlimon Lead Mining Company Limited was incorporated with a capital of £8,000 in eighty £100 shares. Eight of the nine original directors lived in Birmingham (an unfortunately typical feature of Welsh industry) and the company's registered office was located there, as were most of its shareholders. Their high hopes of a quick profit were soon dashed, owing to problems of extraction and transport, which they were too detached to comprehend. The company went into voluntary liquidation on 17 May 1870, after a special resolution passed by the board on 28 April. However, out of the ashes of this company was formed another; The Plynlimon Mining Company Limited, which was incorporated on 26 April 1870. This company had a much higher working capital of £27,000 in 12,000 shares of £2.5s.0d. each; no mean sum in 1870. Similarly, four of the five original directors were English, from London this time, where the registered office was situated. This company too was quickly choked to death by the mud and ruts which blocked the route of its carts and pack-horses over the mountains to rail or coastal outlets.

A leading figure in the local mining and quarrying industry was Captain John Davies of Talybont. In 1889 he become associated, in his plans to exploit the area's natural wealth, with a Mr Thomas Molyneux, Snr, of Earlestown, Lancashire. Molyneux possessed the necessary capital to extend Davies' workings and he was well aware of the value of rail transport to take the ore out of the mountains. The value of the horse drawn tramway, in increasing the output of remote workings, had been known for many years. It was epitomised by the construction of the Festiniog Railway (to the north) to a nominal two feet gauge in the 1830s and 1840s; the narrowness of the gauge greatly reducing the cost of construction. Many other lines followed; those of interest to this history being the horse drawn Corris Railway of 1859 (2ft 3in gauge) and the nearby Talyllyn Railway (also 2ft 3in gauge) which was built in 1865 and designed for steam traction from the outset. The Festiniog made history when it was converted to steam in 1863 (the first use of steam on so narrow a gauge) and the Corris followed suit in 1879. Meanwhile, the standard gauge Aberystwyth and Welsh Coast Railway had been completed in the summer of 1864 (it was absorbed into the Cambrian Railways on 5 July 1865) and proved itself an important factor in opening up the heart of Wales. However, running as it did so close to the coast, it was of little assistance to the mines at the head of the Leri valley. The only hope of regular prosperity would be a railway in the valley itself.

On 8 September 1890, John Davies wrote to Col. Williams (the representative of the Gogerddan estate, which owned large tracts of land in the valley) on behalf of Molyneux, enclosing three ordnance sheets on which had been marked the proposed course of a tramway linking Llanfihangel Station with various mines in the Camdwr Valley in which Molyneux had financial interests. The route was also to serve the Hafan Quarry, Bwlch-glâs lead mine and local farming interests. Molyneux did not consider the large scale extraction of stone from the quarry to be commercially viable without the construction of a tramway to provide economical transport. He was attempting to develop a number of the local workings including Hafan and Henfwlch mines*, for which he acquired the lease on 1 July 1889 (his first venture in the area), Bryn-yr-afr (Hill of the Goats), Camdwr-bâch, Esgair-hîr, Esgair-fraith and, to the south of Talybont, the Elgar mine. He was, it seems, something of a novice in the mining field and many of these mines had been long since worked out. For example, the Hafan mine, as we have seen, had ceased production in 1864 having been worked continuously since 1698. Similarly, Esgair-hîr had first been worked in 1690 (and Esgair-fraith soon afterwards) by a company established by Sir Carbery Pryse of Gogerddan, and the production of lead from the joint mines had peaked in 1856 when 516 tons were produced. The only figures we have for Molyneux's time are 1891 25 tons, 1896 30 tons and 1899 27 tons. By 1900 the output had sunk to 1 ton. The records of the production of copper at Esgair-hîr and Esgair-fraith show a similar situation with a peak of 400 tons in 1880. No figures exist for the period of Molyneux's tenure (and perhaps no copper was produced) but in 1886 it was down to 37 tons and in 1901 it was 46 tons. Both mines finally closed in 1904. Consequently Molyneux was investing large sums of money for a very small return and the more his cash disappeared down these holes in the ground, the more loathe he was to acknowledge his mistake, although he was having serious doubts as to the value of Henfwlch as early as January 1890. In the eighteen months to December 1890, he spent some £2,000 on developing the mines, for practically no return. By July 1891 this figure had risen to £3,500. He was still 'no nearer any income from it' and, according to Capt. Davies, he was 'very sore' about the inaccuracy of the 'flourishing reports' he had received from the previous owners.

The tramway proposal was getting nowhere owing to disagreements with the estate and others as to land prices and its route. Molyneux's finances were stretched still further when his brother, in America, was ruined by a disastrous fire and he wrote frequently to the estate asking for reductions in his rents. On 6 October 1891 Molyneux wrote to Col. Williams,

> I was in London yesterday, trying again to interest some Capitalists in the tramway, but met with a very poor reception. They declared that the Landlords were too grasping [and] that they offered no encouragement...I have tried and tried till I am almost tired but I want to make one more effort and if this fails, then I have done with it.

Molyneux appealed to the estate for assistance in the opening up of the valley, with the assurance that rewards would be reaped in the future, and the estate responded by agreeing to grant the land for the tramway free of charge, where the route traversed their property, in return for royalties on the tonnage carried.

Early in 1892, Molyneux was astounded to find that he did not

* Communication between the Hafan and Henfwlch mine was by carrier pigeon. The Hafan Mine employed twelve men at 18s. per week.

possess the water rights at Hafan, where water power was needed for the dressing of stone. These rights were owned by a Mr Vaughan Davies who demanded too high a price for them. Molyneux proposed to overcome this problem by leasing the Talybont mine (which lies directly above Talybont village) from the estate at a nominal rent and taking the raw ore to be dressed there. Thus, the value of Davies' rights would drop and they could be purchased later. This water problem was the more galling as Molyneux had previously been deprived of a water supply at Elgar where it had been cut off out of sheer malice. The problem lingered on and, in June, Molyneux proposed that he and the estate share the cost of constructing a water course from the Upper Rheidol River. At the same time he modified his plans for the tramway and proposed an extension to the sea, either at Ynyslas or Clarach in order to avoid having to pay the main line 10s. per ton for carriage. He noted that the North Wales quarries were only paying 3s.6d. per ton for water carriage. He was prepared for litigation with the Cambrian over the crossing of their line but considered that the tramway would not be worth building if it only went to Llanfihangel. 'This', he wrote to Col. Williams on 18 July 1892, 'has been the experience of the little line at Dinas Mawddy...and I perceive that this will be the fate of the one I have projected'. Again, on 20 July, 'We shall try first of all to get under the Cambrian bridge at Ynyslas by laying some rails and thus test whether the Cambrian intend to combat, of course there will be a branch to Llanfihangel for passengers and local traffic for stone. If the Cambrian combat, Clarach route will have to be taken'. It had become obvious by this time that the Hafan and Henfwlch mines and the Hafan Quarry alone would supply the line with traffic as the Bryn-yr-afr output was dropping off and the directors had no interest in supplying money for the construction of a tramway and, at this time, the Bwlch-glâs mine was not being worked. Molyneux proposed to lay the first rails on Bank Holiday Monday, 1 August 1892, and requested Sir Pryse Pryse (the owner of the Gogerddan estate) or Lady Pryse to officiate. Col. Williams curtly informed him that 'no rail can be laid on Sir Pryse's land until a contract for the purchase of the same has been entered into'.

On 10 August 1892, Col. Williams received a letter from a Mr Hugh Hughes, Solicitor of Aberystwyth, which ran as follows:

> Mr Molyneux wishes me to assist him to form a strong syndicate of himself and friends to: (1) Construct a Tramway from Havan *[sic]* to the sea. (2) To work Havan stone. (3) To work the Havan and Henfwlch mines if water power can be obtained for that purpose. In the meantime a tunnel is being driven thro' Havan Hill with a view to extending the Tramway to Bryn-yr-afr Mine.

In fact there is no evidence to show that this tunnel was ever commenced, despite a report of February 1897 that it was to be used, in truncated form, to develop the Hafan mine. Another letter from Hughes on 18 August, agreed that the question of the extension to Ynyslas or Clarach should be put into abeyance until the line had been successfully constructed to Llanfihangel and terms for the construction of the tramway were eventually formulated with the estate on 20 September 1892.

CHAPTER FOUR

CONSOLIDATION

1893–1895

As we have seen, Molyneux was well aware of the need for a coastal outlet for his tramway; a need which had been amplified by the refusal of the LNWR to allow the North Wales Narrow Gauge Railways to cross their line in the 1870s. Thus, the NWNGR could not gain access to shipping at Caernarvon and were forced to transfer their goods on to the main line. Such transhipments were very labour intensive and led to the closure, or conversion, of many a narrow gauge railway when the cost of labour rose after the Great War.

The Plynlimon line would be faced with exactly the same problem if they were not permitted to cross the Cambrian Railways and Molyneux made great efforts to do so (despite his agreement with the estate to wait until the line was built to Llanfihangel) as can be seen from his letters of 4 February and 14 March 1893

> ...until outlet to the sea is provided...I shall not lay a yard and therefore they too will be loosers by being obdurate...I am not going to be at the mercy of the Rail Co for I perceive that by getting to the sea, the stone is capable of making a large industry, but it will be simply throttled or choked, by being restricted to [the main] line...I shall be compelled to go to Clarach (which they cannot prevent) if passage to Ynyslas is not arranged.
>
> The negotiations with the Cambrian have resulted in nothing. We have surveyed the Lerry and...Capt. Davies will send you the tracing to Borth...Borth will do just as well for us for discharging into the Railway trucks as Llanfihangel and we can get to the sea by barges on the river, with a little dredging.

On 17 March, Col. Williams wrote to Molyneux, 'I regret to hear that you cannot arrange with the Cambrian Railways as to terms of entering Llanfihangel Station'. By the beginning of April the Cambrian had refused permission for their line to be crossed at any point; an indication of the fierce competition for traffic which existed between the private railway companies in those days. Consequently plans were deposited, in a letter dated 18 April 1893 from Capt. Davies to Col. Williams, for a tramway from Hafan to a farm by the name of Brynllys. The farm lies just over one mile south-east of Borth station on the eastern bank of the Leri. The route was subject to Sir Pryse Pryse's permission as he owned this land also. The letter added,

> ...Below that [Brynllys] we have not quite decided which side of the Lerry to take, but the plans of the remaining portion will be sent as soon as possible.

These remaining plans were to continue the line down to Ynyslas and dispatch the goods by barge, under the Cambrian Railways, to a wharf on the River Dovey. There they would be offloaded into waiting ships. A branch to Llanfihangel would be included if terms could be agreed with the Cambrian. These plans appear to have been modified very quickly for, by 26 April, Molyneux was seriously considering the purchase of a fleet of barges to be used between the south end of the canalised section of the Leri, just north of Brynllys, and the Dovey, rather than run the tramway to Ynyslas. Rocks and old tree trunks were removed from the river with this in view. The next day Molyneux wrote a further letter to the estate, stating that, 'The bed of the line, on the Common land, is almost completed' (this being the land just to the east of Talybont) and over forty men were engaged on the works at this time. This brought a sudden rebuff from the estate, saying that Sir Pryse Pryse could not agree to the plans until the exact course of the line was decided upon and the necessary agreements drawn up. Thus, all work come to a halt on 29 April 1893 and Molyneux lost a large order for paving setts. Molyneux appears to have considered this seemingly rational demand as the last straw and a letter of 5 May, from Mr Hugh Hughes to Col. Williams, stated that Molyneux was 'prepared to withdraw from his connection with the projected tramway in favour of Capt. John Davies and his friends' and that Davies had managed to persuade the Cambrian to allow them to enter Llanfihangel station. In the event Molyneux did not withdraw and he agreed, once more, to limit his plans to a terminus at Llanfihangel. Although he had grave doubts as to the economic viability of a tramway without a coastal outlet, his chief concern was to provide an outlet for his mines.

Negotiations on the exact course of the line, the water supply at Hafan and Henfwlch and other matters went unresolved through the rest of 1893 and into 1894 with, at one point, the estate considering quashing the tramway proposals completely. Things went from bad to worse and, in June 1894, Molyneux was served with a writ to restrain him from removing stone from the Hafan Quarry, which the estate claimed he was not entitled to do. Other problems included various claims for damage to land, crops and drainage as a result of those sections of the trackbed which had already been constructed. On 13 November 1894, Capt. Davies presented Col. Williams with new plans for the tramway from Llanfihangel to Hafan. Davies observes, in a letter of 22 November, that,

> As far as I know the only section in dispute is the one from Talybont to the middle of Glanfraed farm. It is therefore a question as to whether we go through Pantycalch Gap or under Tyncae farmhouse...To follow the road all the way from Llanfihangel to Talybont would be impossible for a Horse Tramway as it would require a long tunnel from Nant-y-Groglwyd to the middle of Talybont Hill and there would be impossible curves to contend with.

The estate appeared to be looking on the tramway more favourably at this juncture and Molyneux was eager for a speedy settlement as he wished to visit his brother, in America, early in the new year; a trip that was to be put off several times. Articles of Agreement with Sir Pryse Pryse were drawn up on 4 February 1895 but other negotiations dragged on all through the year and by December Molyneux was again talking of extending to Ynyslas. On 14 December he received a letter from the Board of Trade, granting his application to make use of the foreshore at Ynyslas. He states (in a letter to Pryse Pryse Pryse Esq, Sir Pryse Pryse's eldest son, who had a hand in the management of the estate)

> ...we now know that Hafan Stone can be made to accommodate 700 men, at an average output of 3 tons per man per week and it is to the interest of the whole community that the output be made as large as possible.

Finally, after five years determined struggle by Molyneux, Deeds of Conveyance (of land for the tramway) were drawn up with Sir Pryse Pryse, Messrs Herbert Vaughan and Price Lewis and Mr P. P. Pryse, on the last day of 1895. Two thirds of the route was over land leased from the Gogerddan estate. Thus, early in the new year, the construction was re-commenced in earnest.

CHAPTER FIVE

CONSTRUCTION

1896

With the coming of the new year, Col. Williams disappeared from the scene and Mr Pryse Pryse Pryse took over the day to day running of the estate. This change caused Molyneux much relief as he considered, justifiably, that Williams had been unnecessarily obstructive towards the tramway proposals. On Saturday 11 January 1896, a small and quiet ceremony was to be held to cut the first sod. As it was, the news of the occasion quickly circulated, a large crowd gathered and the event was reported at length in *The Aberystwyth Observer* (16 January 1896):

THE TALYBONT TRAMWAY

CUTTING THE FIRST SOD
BY MR PRYSE PRYSE

For some four years negotiations have been pending between Mr Molyneux, Earlestown, Lancashire, who is locally represented by his agent, Capt. John Davies, on the one hand, and Sir Pryse Pryse, the genial baronet of Gogerddan, and other landlords, on the other hand, for the purpose of securing land for the construction of a tramway between Llanfihangel Geneu'rglyn station on the Cambrian Railways, and the Havan Sett Quarry and mines, which are situated some five miles beyond Talybont, in the direction of Plynlimon mountain. The land belongs chiefly to Sir Pryse Pryse, but owing to his absence abroad the negotiations had to be conducted with his agent. Last year the management of the Gogerddan estate was taken over by Sir Pryse's eldest son, Mr Pryse Pryse, Lodge Park. Realising that the tramway would not only benefit Mr Molyneux and the estate, but also the community in the district, Mr Pryse entered heartily into the spirit of the project, and he has, on behalf of himself and his father, given every encouragement to the promoters. Other landlords had to be negotiated with, and some difficulties were experienced, but all have now been amicably overcome. It may be said that Mr Molyneux deserves the best thanks of the community for his enterprise, and particularly for the plucky persistence with which he has grappled with the initial difficulties. But, as he says, he has great confidence in the quarry, and hopes to be handsomely rewarded for time, labour, and capital. It is also impossible not to give a word of praise to Captain John Davies, who has laboured in season and out of season in promoting the scheme, and who has prepared all the plans and surveys. The setts produced from the quarry are remarkably good, indeed it may be said that they are equal to anything to be found in the kingdom. The stones are very hard, and yet easily worked. The Aberystwyth Town Council have used them for street crossings, and will no doubt require more when they can be easily delivered in the town. Not long ago a cargo was sent into Lancashire by the steamer Countess of Lisburne, and an offer was in consequence made to Mr Molyneux to supply 1,000 tons. The order could not, however, be accepted, because of the great cost of carriage from the quarry to the sea. When the tramway is completed this difficulty will be removed. It is said that in a short time five hundred men can be employed in the quarry, and this would enable a large number of men who have been obliged to go to the South Wales coal mines for work to return to their native homes. By means of a tunnel another valley can be entered in which are several lead mines, which are now closed. With somewhat better prices and cheaper transit some if not all of these mines will no doubt be re-opened, to the great benefit of the workmen, the promoters, and the landlords. Here we may say that Mr Pryse Pryse, with the sanction of his father, is prepared to give good terms to those who may be desirous of re-opening the mines on the Gogerddan estate, provided they can show bona fide intentions. In the past the terms insisted upon by agents have done much to destroy the mining industry in North Cardiganshire. There have, of course, been honourable exceptions. For the present the tramway, which will be worked by locomotives, will only carry goods, the Board of Trade requirements being such as to make it impossible to adapt the line for passenger traffic. This is very much to be regretted, for a passenger line would prove of immense value to the inhabitants of Talybont and Bontgoch, with such adjacent villages as Tre'rddol and Taliesin, in addition to the scattered population of the district. It is hoped, however, that under the coming Light Railways Bill these restrictions will be very much modified. In that case no doubt thousands of visitors from Aberystwyth, Borth, and elsewhere, would in the summer time travel over the line, which passes through a beautiful country. It has been suggested, and the suggestion meets with universal favour in the district, that the line should be made of the ordinary width between Llanfihangel and Talybont, and narrow gauge afterwards, and we are authorised to state that the suggestion will be borne in mind, and if it is feasible a third rail will be laid, so as to be available for rolling stock of either width.

It is intended to continue the tramway to Ynyslas on the Dovey, a distance of five miles, and also to ship some of the setts at Aberystwyth.

All the deeds and documents having been signed, sealed and delivered, it was at the end of last week decided that the first sod should be cut on Saturday, and Mr Pryse Pryse kindly consented to perform that function, and on Saturday morning a few friends were invited to be

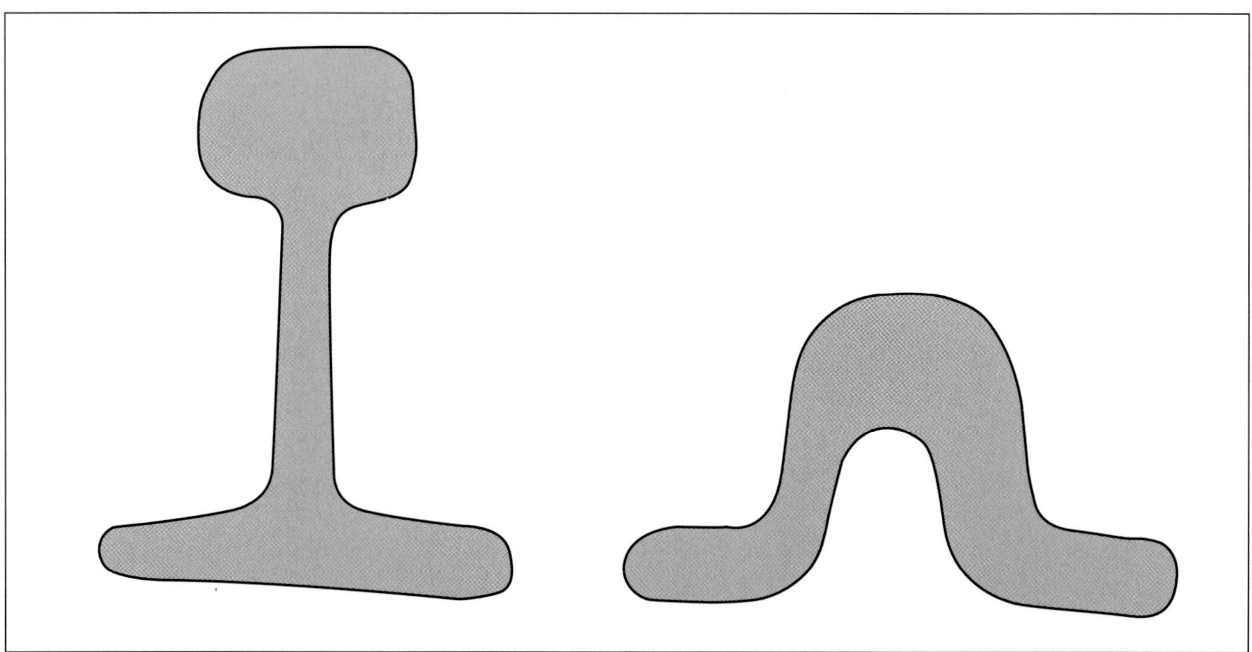

Full size sections of the main line, flat bottom rail (left) and extension bridge rail (right).

present at the ceremony, which was intended to be of an unostentatious nature. A small party went up from Aberystwyth, Mr Pryse drove in from Lodge Park, and Mr Molyneux arrived from Lancashire, and at three o'clock they proceeded to a field on a hill a little to the south of the village, where a flag had just been erected. Small as the party was at the start, by the time they reached the field it had been joined by scores of persons of all ages, including leading inhabitants, a few of whom had come some miles - so mysteriously does news travel in the country - and finally a big crowd had assembled.

At the invitation of Mr Molyneux, Mr Pryse Pryse took the spade which had been provided, and in a few well-chosen sentences, said that he felt greatly honoured by having been asked to perform that ceremony. The tramway would benefit the Gogerddan estate and the whole community, and he wished it every success. Mr Pryse then cut the sod, and was loudly cheered. He added that he would keep the spade in memory of the interesting event.

Capt. Davies said he was sorry that it was not a silver spade.

Mr Molyneux thanked Mr Pryse for kindly coming there to cut the sod, and hoped the tramway will benefit the Gogerddan estate and the whole community. He would do his best to ensure success. He also thanked Capt. John Davies, Mr Peter Jones, the representative of the Aberystwyth Observer, and all present. He had only expected to find two or three present. (Applause.)

Capt. Davies said that the scheme ought to benefit Aberystwyth, and especially the harbour.

Mr Peter Jones expressed his gratification at being present on so interesting an occasion. The tramway would establish a connection which was greatly needed between different parts of the district, and would also be an incentive to other districts. For this they were greatly indebted to Mr Molyneux. (Hear hear.) Light railways meant many difficulties, the chief of which were the securing of money and traffic. The former would be overcome by Mr Molyneux, and they were assured of the success of the scheme. Expensive traffic was a check upon business. There was an unlimited supply of setts at Havan, and with the cheap means of transit provided by the tramway the enterprise would be a commercial success. It would be an advantage to the whole district. The quarry would keep the workmen in their native air, a much healthier atmosphere than they found in South Wales, (Applause) and a large number would be employed. The scheme would have a wide effect in the district, and would prove an advantage, through the shipment of the setts, to Aberystwyth. There was an identity of interests. As an individual member he thought he might say that the Town Council will do all that they can to make the enterprise a success, and the County Council will also treat Mr Molyneux in the best way it can. He admired Mr Molyneux's great pertinacity, which deserved success. He proposed their heartiest thanks to Mr Pryse. Landlords have rights and duties as well as privileges, and Mr Pryse realised that, and therefore he was glad to see him there. He hoped the spade would remind Mr Pryse of that day, and that he would find it of utility in the future. (Laughter and loud cheers.)

Mr Pryse said no thanks were needed. He felt they had done him a great honour, and thought the enterprise is bound to succeed. (Applause.)

Mr Molyneux said he was very much obliged for the kindly references to himself and the scheme. The engine which is to work the tram is being constructed, and will be ready in three or four months.

Capt. Davies said he hoped to be able to give them a ride when the line is

> completed, and was glad to see so many present.
>
> After general congratulations the proceedings terminated, and the crowd returned to the village, Mr Pryse proudly carrying the spade on his shoulder.
>
> Afterwards a well-served tea, with ham and eggs, was provided at the White Lion Hotel. Among those who sat down at the table were Mr Pryse Pryse, Mr Molyneux, Dr James, Alderman Peter Jones, Mr John Morgan, Mr Philip, Capt. Northey, Mr Northey, Esgairhir, Capt. John Davies, &c.
>
> On parting Mr Molyneux thanked Mr Pryse and other gentlemen for their presence, Mr Pryse briefly responded, and Capt. Davies having remarked that they hoped to have a substantial dinner when the line is opened, the day's proceedings were brought to a close.

It should, perhaps, be made clear that the third line of the title of this article, 'BY MR PRYSE PRYSE', refers to Mr Pryse cutting the first sod and did not mean to imply that Mr Pryse wrote the article; a circumstance which would throw a rather different light on it. Later that year Mr Molyneux presented him with a small silver spade to commemorate the occasion.

It is clear from this article that the company still planned to obtain access to the sea, via Ynyslas, and on the day the article was published (16 January) Molyneux, who had returned to Earlestown, wrote to the Chief Engineer of the Cambrian Railways in a further attempt to reach an amicable agreement. The letter ran...

> I beg you to accept [an] ordnance Map on which is traced the route of the tram line, the bed of which is now in course of preparation. I think it is also desirable to place you and the Directors of the Cambrian Railway Co, in possession of a few details respecting the districts the tram line will tap, for I then feel sure that cordial co-operation will result, in spite of the fact that the line will connect with the Sea direct, because such added industry cannot fail to benefit the Cambrian Co both directly and indirectly. The statements which I append are not overdraw by any means... .

Attached to this letter was a brief outline of Molyneux's intentions for the exploitation of the mineral wealth of the area which stated that the...

> Plynlimon and Talybont Tramway, will tap the richest and most prolific Metalliferous zone in Cardiganshire. (These are the words of the late Sir Warrington Smythe & I emphasize them). It will be laid from Llanfihangel to Hafan Hill via Talybont first; next a branch to Ynyslas on the Dovey to a point about opposite Aberdovey Hotel. Hafan Valley contains nine at least lead and copper deposits, at least three slate beds and the hill of valuable stone, all of which are at present dormant. All of the foregoing I have secured with the exception of three, and I believe I shall get these as well. My opinion is that Welsh lead Mining must be conducted on a completely changed plan of operations, viz, grouping where deposits lend themselves conveniently for the purpose. These in this valley lend themselves admirably to the plan, for the lodes run parallel along both sides [of] the route of the tram line, thus enabling concentration of management and dressing. The great curse of Welsh Lead Mining has been over-capitalization and extrav[ag]ance. I can work all this group with a capital (Line included) that has usually been floated for a single one.

Molyneux concluded by praising the quality and ease of cleavage of Hafan stone, asserting that, 'Over two miles of galleries can be made, which at 5 yards per man means 700 men independent of all other hands' and that 'the

Cambrian Co cannot fail to reap largely from such large accession of industry.' In the course of the sod cutting ceremony Captain Davies had suggested the extension of the line from Llanfihangel to Aberystwyth Harbour; which, he considered, would benefit both Talybont and Aberystwyth. It is doubtful that the Cambrian Railways board would have smiled on the suggestion, as such an extension would have had to be built parallel to their own line. However, such an outlet would probably have given the tramway greater chance of survival than an outlet at Ynyslas and certainly a better chance than no sea outlet at all, but the financial interests of the Cambrian clearly lay in forcing the Plynlimon and Hafan to tranship at Llanfihangel.

Construction started in earnest on Monday morning (13 January) and by the close of February between forty and fifty men were at work on the track bed. The promoters published a four page pamphlet entitled 'A brief description of the Plynlimon and Hafan Narrow Guage *[sic]* 2ft. 3in. Tramline, and the district it traverses and will serve.' The local lead mining industry was at a low ebb at this time and this pamphlet sought to stimulate geological interest in the valley, thus providing more traffic for the tramway. Molyneux was well aware of the value of publicity and was quick to note that the Prince of Wales (the future King Edward VII) was due to visit Aberystwyth in mid-June 1896. He was to be installed as Chancellor of the University of Wales and an attempt was made to complete at least a section of the line with a view to a royal opening. In the event, however, a space could not be found in the royal diary and the idea never materialised.

Having no previous experience of such a venture, the estate took the step, in March 1896 of entering into correspondence with the Glyn Valley Tramway Co. at Chirk. Various information was solicited regarding rates and tariffs suitable for such

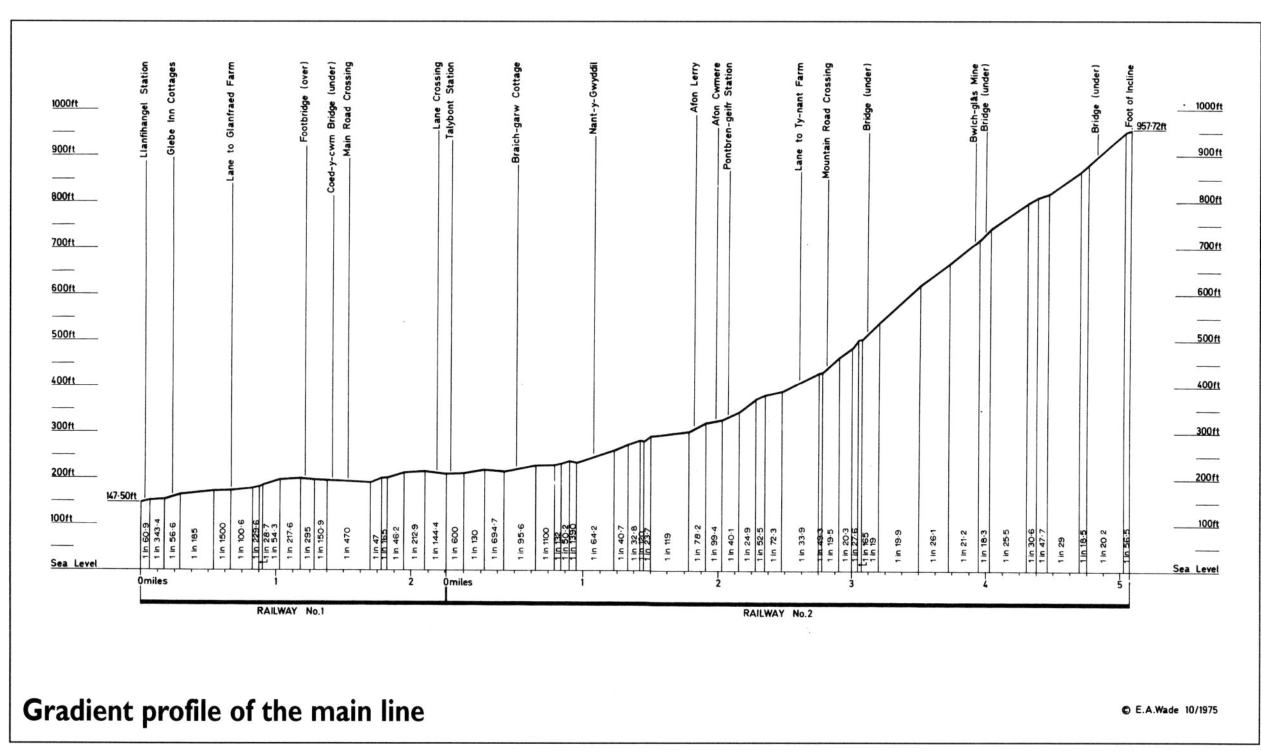

Gradient profile of the main line

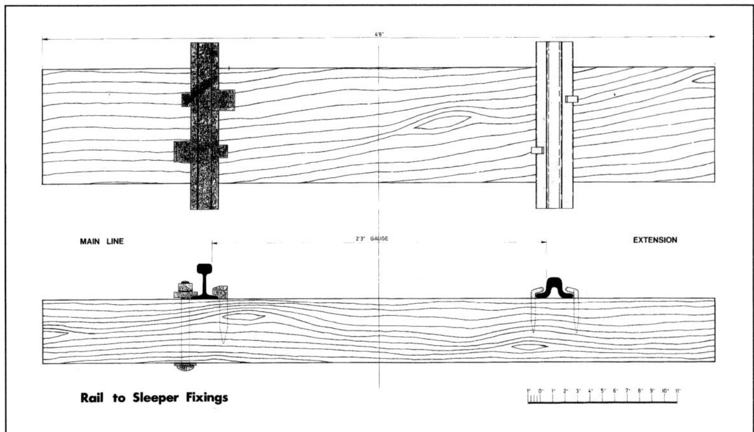

Rail to sleeper fixings

tramways. On 22 April, Molyneux wrote to Mr P. P. Pryse to ask him to persuade the local farmers to let him have their unwanted hay seeds, so that he might sow the edges of the trackbed for appearance sake. In March or April 1896, Molyneux appears to have obtained the lease of the Cwmere Quarry, just to the south of Pontbren-geifr, to which he proposed to build a branch of the tramway. In a letter dated 11 May 1896, he states, 'I would like the Cwmerai branch so arranged that the loco might be able to get up to the bottom gallery'. The line was expected to be complete by June 1897 and there was talk of a standard gauge extension into Talybont. There were also rumours of plans for an official passenger service on the tramway, as Molyneux had, for some time, been aware of the financial value of tourists. This plan was to materialise later, albeit in a very restricted form.

Early in July 1896, Molyneux received a shock when his associate in the venture, Captain Davies, died at the early age of fifty-six, leaving him to carry out their plans alone. Molyneux wrote (in a letter to Mr P. P. Pryse, dated 3 July 1896) 'I have feared it for some time, for the drink has made terrible havoc of him of late, and in fact it has been a tremendous expensive matter for me. I did not like to discharge him and in a certain sense I am now glad that I did not, for if his death had occurred after I had done so, it would have been more or less a matter of regret to me'. In the same letter he asked for Mr Pryse's opinion of a Capt. Williams as a successor to Davies. The funeral was performed on 6 July and on 9 July Molyneux wrote to Mr Pryse, 'We are now making good progress and I regret that I did not remove Capt. Davies before'. Other business commitments tended to keep Molyneux in Lancashire for most of his time and he found it expedient to send his son, Thomas Molyneux, Jnr, to live at Gwynfa, Talybont, to keep an eye on things.

Molyneux appears to have also had certain financial worries at this time. In a letter dated 1 September 1896, he suggested to Mr P. P. Pryse that the introduction of a passenger carriage to the tramway would attract additional revenue, and for most of the year he had been attempting to form a syndicate to assist him in the running of the mines and the tramway. Then, on 9 September, Molyneux sent Mr Hugh Hughes a long and depressing letter which ran as follows:

> Up to yesterday I had hoped that something still remained in the stone whereby the Syndicate could go on but the wires from my son has now dispelled all hope. It will be necessary that Sir Pryse see this letter in order to fully understand the position. When it was discovered at Capt. Davies' death how cruelly he had wronged by falsifying the sheets and misleading me about the stone I immediately took steps to see what could be done and it has taken all this time to get to the bottom of it...the great expected output cannot be produced yet...and therefore a large Company is out of the question. I am now trying to form a syndicate for the group of mines and to add the stone as an auxiliary along with the line. Also in

> addition and as an extra attraction trying to induce extension to Plynlimmon [*sic*] so that tourists and visitors may assist to bring in returns. I mention these things so that it may be seen that I have been and am doing all I can to avoid abandoning the scheme. I need scarcely say that for me it is a terrible crusher, a loss of over £10,000. First there was £1,200 for Hafan and Henfwlch..all there was realised was £58...I can spend no more. My means are exhausted and more the strain has been terribly severe, disappointment following disappointment in spite of all my efforts and now I want a rest preparatory to hard work to help to make up for this great loss for I shall not sit down under it.

And sit down he did not for, on 24 October 1896, the Plynlimon and Hafan Company Limited was incorporated with a nominal capital of £30,000 in three-thousand shares of £10 each. It was set up with the object, among other things, of 'acquiring from Mr Thomas Molyneux, Senior, of 41, Market Street, Earlestown, Warrington, Lancashire, Manufacturer, certain lands, quarries, mines, mineral rights and other property within the County of Cardigan, and to carry on the business of quarry proprietors and stone and slate merchants'.

Section 3 of the Articles of Incorporation (the section with direct reference to the tramway) stated...

> d) to construct, purchase, lease or otherwise acquire any (local) tramway or tramways...
>
> e) to equip and to maintain and to work by electricity, steam, cable, horse or other mechanical or animal power all tramways and railways belonging or leased to the Company or in which the Company may be interested.
>
> f) to carry on the business of tramway, railway, carriage, omnibus and van proprietors and carriers of passengers and goods by land and water...

One can see from these articles that Molyneux was well aware of the advantages of steam power but nevertheless wise enough to keep his options open. The first directors were, in alphabetical order, William Benjamin Bowring (Liverpool), John William Davidson (Liverpool), Harry Johnson Houghton (Earlestown), Thomas Molyneux, Snr (Earlestown), John Slee (Earlestown), William Thomson (Liverpool) and Charles Thomas Whitley (Warrington). Not one Welshman among them! An agreement, dated 2 November 1896, between Molyneux and the newly formed company stated:

> The Vendor has acquired or agreed to acquire certain leases or mining rights in respect of certain quarries, mines and minerals situate at the Hafan Hill and elsewhere in the County of Cardigan and has acquired or agreed to acquire for the purpose of constructing a tramway or railway from the said quarries and mines to Llanfihangel Station and whereas the Vendor has commenced to work the said quarries and to construct the said tramway or railway and to carry on the business of a quarry proprietor, it is hereby agreed that the Vendor shall sell and the Company shall purchase.
>
> Consideration for the sale shall be £14,000 which shall be satisfied by allotment to the Vendor or his nominee/s of 1,400 fully paid up ordinary shares of £10 each.
>
> The Company shall take over the said business and premises from June 6, 1896.

We are not informed how many shares each of the other directors acquired but Molyneux, with his 46.6%, retained at least the major holding. Consequently, he became Managing Director as from the date of the

Agreement (2 November 1896) whilst Thomas, Jnr, was installed as General Manager and Engineer at the end of the year. The Deputy Manager was a Mr James Halliday and the company adopted a simple Corporate Seal, 1⅝ inch in diameter, consisting of a monogram encircled by the full title. The first Secretary to the company was a Mr W. A. Davidson of Messrs J. W. Davidson, Cookson and Co., Chartered Accountants of 48 Castle Street, Liverpool. J. W. Davidson, it will be noted, was a member of the Board. Mr Frank H. Stables, of the same firm, became the second and last Secretary, in March 1898. The registered office was also at 48 Castle Street but moved to number 26 in June 1897 and to number 6 a year later; presumably following moves by the accountants. The company solicitors were Messrs Alsop, Stevens, Harvey and Crooks, of 14 Castle Street, Liverpool.

A letter of 22 November 1896, from Molyneux to Mr P. P. Pryse, observes that the delivery of the rails and sleepers to Llanfihangel was expected on 7 or 8 December 1896. It goes on to state his opinion that one passenger carriage would suffice for the potential passenger traffic and that another could be purchased later if it should be required. Another letter followed on 7 December to say that Molyneux was 'trying to arrange with the Gilbertson family to run a branch through their land to Elgar'. A previous letter, of 13 July, had suggested that this line would run to the Elgar mine via the Cefn-gwyn mine and the south-west end of Cwmere Quarry, which Molyneux was already working, but it was never constructed. A letter of 9 December ran...'May I presume you will grant us land to extend from Bryn-yr-afr to Esgair-hîr* and try to get Sir James Szlumper to adopt our gauge of 2ft 3in for the proposed Devils Bridge line'. This was the Aberystwyth to Devil's Bridge, Vale of Rheidol Railway, which was opened in 1902. Obviously, Molyneux still had ideas of gaining a direct coastal outlet by extending to Aberystwyth harbour in which event it would have made sense to share gauges and facilities with the Rheidol. It seems that the Board of the Vale of Rheidol Railway seriously considered adopting the 2ft 3in gauge but eventually settled for 1 foot 11½ inches as it would give them slightly more flexibility on their tenuous mountain route.

It is interesting, at this juncture, to reflect on why the 2ft 3in gauge was chosen for the Hafan line. The quick answer is that its neighbours, the Corris and Talyllyn Railways, were of that gauge and it seems quite rational to follow suit. However, it should be noted that, about this time, there were plans to link the two systems to the north, via Talyllyn Lake. At the southern end of the Corris there was an old extension to Derwenlas (rendered obsolete by the building of the Cambrian Railways) and this ended a mere seven miles from Talybont. It is quite possible that Molyneux had dreams of linking all four systems; after all, that is exactly what Charles Easton Spooner was doing at that time with the two foot gauge lines in Caernarvonshire.

Be that as it may, the rough formation of the trackbed had been completed as far as the foot of the Hafan Incline by 15 December 1896 and there were high hopes for an opening early in the new year.

* The proposed branches, via a tunnel through the Hafan Hill, to the Bryn-yr-afr and Esgair-hîr mines never materialised. It is doubtful that they would have much prolonged the life of the tramway as the Esgair-hîr was closed in January 1904, under the direction of the Cardiganshire Consolidated Mining Co. Ltd. However, the Bryn-yr-afr was worked continuously from 1881 until 1912, with the exception of 1909.

CHAPTER SIX

COMPLETION

1897

On 4 January 1897, the rails and sleepers eventually left Merseyside, one month behind schedule. They were taken by sea to Aberdovey Harbour, where they were transhipped on to the Cambrian line and delivered to Llanfihangel, via Glandovey Junction (re-named Dovey Junction in September 1904). The first rails were laid on Monday 11 January, at Talybont, by Thomas Molyneux, Snr, for which purpose they must have been brought from Llanfihangel by road.

The main tramway was 7 miles 26 chains in length (to the foot of the incline) and, for the purposes of construction, was divided into two sections. Railway No 1, Llanfihangel to Talybont (2 miles 21 chains) and Railway No 2, Talybont to the foot of the incline (5 miles 5 chains). The double tracked incline and the extension to the Hafan Quarry, a length of 1½ miles, were dealt with separately. A Mr Price of Newtown, Montgomeryshire, won the contract for the permanent way of, at least, the first section of the tramway. The permanent way for the main line consisted of earth ballast (i.e. local rock chippings) with wooden sleepers, 4ft 6in long by 9ft wide by 5in deep at 3ft centres. The flat bottomed rails weighed about 30lbs per yard and were secured to the sleepers by two dog spikes and two bolts and clips; each pair being set diagonally on each sleeper. Thus, we have a total of eight fixing points on each sleeper; a very substantial method of construction, obviously intended for long usage. On the extension, earth ballast appears to have been used again, with bridge rails of about 20lbs per yard, probably fixed just with dog spikes. The sleepers cost 3d. each and the minimum radius curve was three chains (main line).

By the end of February the rails were laid from Llanfihangel to Talybont (Pen-y-Rhiw) station which was erected in a field of which Mr Morgan, the publican at the White Lion, was the tenant. The ballasting was hastily continued to the foot of the Hafan incline, which was constructed during February and March at a cost, including permanent way, winding drum, etc, of over £500. Work on the extension continued through April and, by the end of the spring, the whole 8 miles 66 chains of tramway was virtually complete.

Corporate seal (full size)

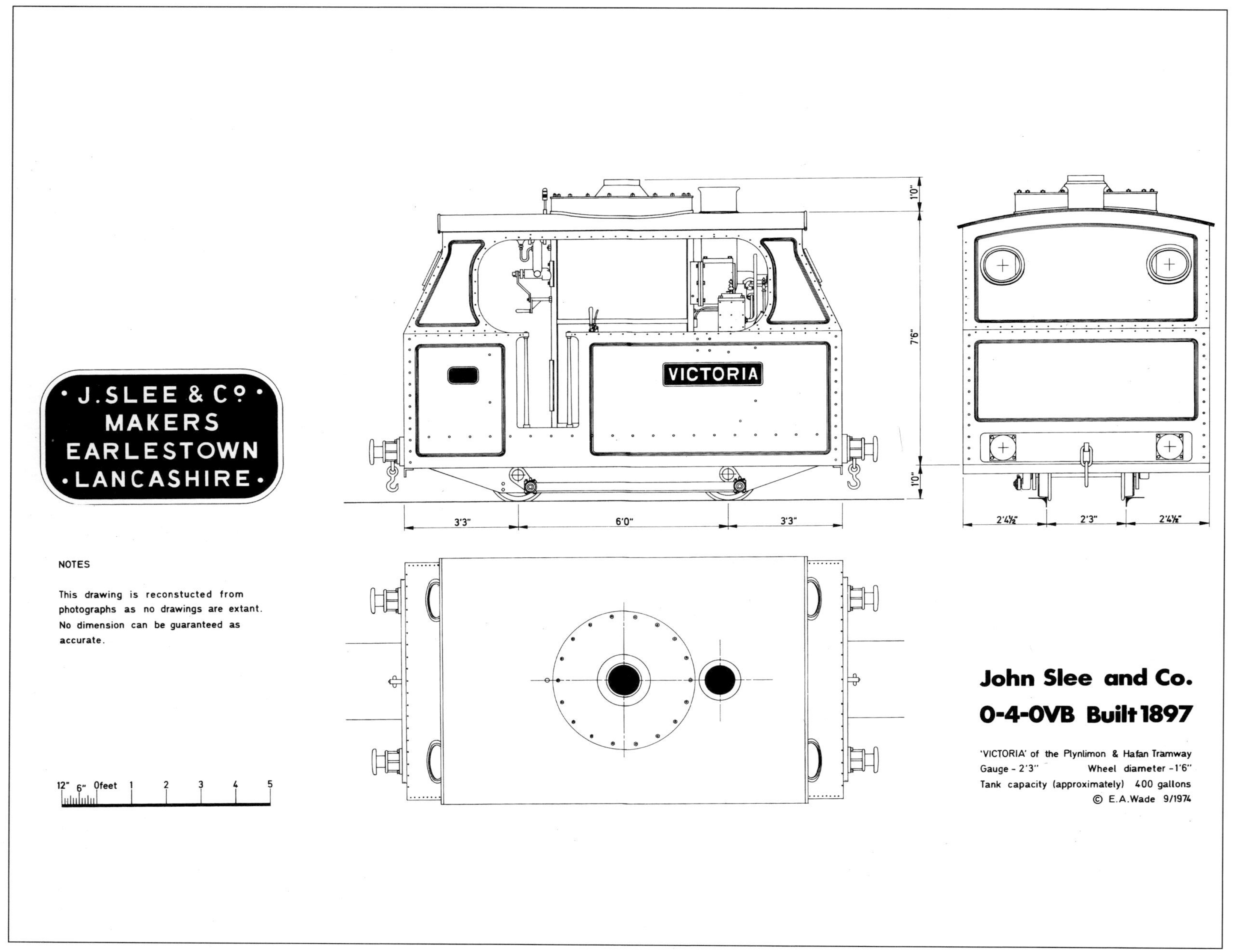
• J.SLEE & C°. •
MAKERS
EARLESTOWN
• LANCASHIRE •
VICTORIA
1'0"
7'6"
1'0"
3'3"
6'0"
3'3"
2'4½"
2'3"
2'4½"
NOTES
This drawing is reconstucted from photographs as no drawings are extant.
No dimension can be guaranteed as accurate.
12" 6" 0feet 1 2 3 4 5
John Slee and Co.
0-4-0VB Built 1897
'VICTORIA' of the Plynlimon & Hafan Tramway
Gauge - 2'3"
Wheel diameter - 1'6"
Tank capacity (approximately) 400 gallons
© E.A.Wade 9/1974

CHAPTER SEVEN

VICTORIA

The first locomotive to do service on the tramway was of very unorthodox design; seemingly owing something to the products of the de Winton Company of Caernarvon. She was built by Messrs John Slee and Co. of the Earlestown Engineering Works, Warrington, in which Molyneux was a partner. John Slee, being a director of the Plynlimon and Hafan Company, this appears to have been an attempt to save some money. It seems that Slee had never made a locomotive before but, considering the uniqueness of the finished product, he must have had some strong opinions on them. He certainly had considerable experience in the manufacture of steam pumping engines, etc. Named *Victoria,* probably inspired by the Diamond Jubilee, she was (like the de Wintons) an 0-4-0 vertical boilered locomotive. Unlike the de Winton engines, *Victoria* had her safety valves mounted centrally, on top of the boiler, with a cranked chimney emerging from the front. She was also fitted with an over-all cab after the fashion of street tram engines.

The Cambrian Railways delivered her to Llanfihangel on Wednesday 12

VICTORIA at Talybont when newly delivered. Note the large vertical boiler with its offset chimney and top mounted safety valve casing. A vertical cylinder is also visible, although the total number of cylinders remains a subject for debate. The identity of the men is unknown but it is tempting to speculate that the bowler hatted man, next to the maker's plate, may be John Slee.
NATIONAL LIBRARY OF WALES

May 1897, where a sizeable crowd was waiting to greet her. After transfer from the main line wagon to her own rails she was made ready for the inaugural trip to Talybont, where another crowd, and a gaily decorated engine shed, were waiting for her. In the event she travelled no further than Glebe Inn Cottages, a mere 22 chains, and then returned down the gradient mainly by gravity. The official reason for the failure was that muddy water had been supplied but this was probably deliberate sabotage and the fire had to be quickly drawn when the injector became clogged with dirt. After spending the night in Llanfihangel she succeeded in reaching Talybont the next day.

Legend has it that she was built with four cylinders, two driving each axle, but that owing to her inability to raise sufficient steam, two of them were disconnected. The photograph of her at Talybont (presumably when first delivered) shows only two cylinders. If there were ever two others it would have left little room for her crew and one would expect to see some evidence of their removal.* She was generally an extremely poor runner and, within three months, the company were forced to purchase another engine to work the line. They went to an established locomotive builder, W. G. Bagnall Ltd, of the Castle Engine Works, Stafford, who just happened to have a suitable replacement engine in stock, which only needed re-gauging. The new loco arrived in August 1897 and *Victoria* could not have run for very long afterwards, if at all. John Slee must have had a very red face at this time and it seems he never made another locomotive. His company went out of business before 1914. A photograph shows the two engines at Pen-y-Rhiw (Talybont) station with *Victoria*, minus wheels and cylinders, resting on timber baulks. She was probably scrapped when the line was finally closed, although it has been suggested that she was sold to a quarry in North Wales.

* In this connection, the reader's attention is drawn to an article by Rodney Weaver which was published in *The Narrow Gauge* (the journal of the Narrow Gauge Railway Society) No 102, Spring 1984. This article and the ensuing correspondence (Nos 104, 108 and 112) is reproduced in full in Appendix 1.

CHAPTER EIGHT

CASUALTIES

It appears that the advent of a steam tramway in the valley was not altogether welcomed by certain sections of the populace. We have already seen evidence of sabotage, in the dirty water provided for *Victoria's* first trip. The next attack was to prove far more serious.

On Friday 4 June 1897, *Victoria* was proceeding with her train, some distance to the west of Coed-y-cwm, when a log was noticed, lying across the track. The engine was able to draw to a halt in time and the obstruction was removed. However, the next day the log was back on the rails again, only this time it was bolted down to a sleeper. That afternoon *Victoria* left Llanfihangel pushing two 'trollies' and pulling a third. On the footplate were Mr David Jones, driver, Evan Davies, fireman and, it is believed, Frederick Simms (a company clerk). On the first trolley sat Messrs James Rowland Jones, Thomas Edwards (of Talybont) and Richard Roberts (also of Talybont). The second trolley was occupied by William Jones and the rear trolley by a further six or seven people; all on a line which had no proper authority to carry passengers! When the train was some fifteen yards from the Glanfred Farm level crossing and travelling, according to the subsequent evidence, at a 'moderate' speed, James Jones and Thomas Edwards noticed the timber fouling the rails. Mr Roberts slid to the end of the beam, which lay across the trolley for the purpose of carrying timber, and, reaching the front of the vehicle, apparently attempted to clear the obstruction. The train gave two violent jerks and Roberts lay dead beneath the locomotive, his companions being thrown clear. Richard Roberts was thirty-five and was employed by the Plynlimon and Hafan Company to work on the tramway.

The funeral was conducted on the following day, by the Rev. E. Jones, in the cemetery of the Independent Chapel and was well attended; Roberts being a popular character locally and a member of various choirs. At the formal inquest on the day of the accident and the adjourned inquest on 9 June, a ganger (Richard Jenkins) said in evidence that the piece of timber was 'an inch thick and a few inches long', and that the rails and locomotive were in good condition. This was affirmed by Mr Rowland Edwards, relayer. It was suggested that it would have been safer had all persons sat on the rear trolley, and the evidence was that there was sufficient room for them. Mr J. B. Morgan of Glanfraed considered that the locomotive did not work properly. Evidence was also given by Thomas Molyneux and his son (the tramway's General Manager and Engineer) and David Jones the driver, following which Mr John Evans, the Coroner, summed up. The jury considered that Robert's death was caused by falling off the trolley as it left the rails in front of the locomotive, but felt that there was no satisfactory evidence to show what had caused the derailment. A full report of the story and the two inquests appeared in the *Cambrian News* on 11 June 1897.

The Company it seems, were blind to the implications of this tragedy with regard to the safety of passengers, for less than two months later another accident occurred. On Monday 2 August Mr and Mrs Jones of Pen-Rhiw, Talybont, were riding on a trolley frame near Braich-garw. Mrs Jones carried her eight-months old daughter, wrapped in a shawl. According to the evidence given at the inquest, and reported in the *Cambrian News* on 6 August 1897 'John Mason Jones, father of the deceased...was returning home with his wife and child and some friends on a trolley worked by sitting on the side and pushing with the feet, when the child which was in its mother's arms fell through the middle of the trolley, which was really only a frame without any planks covering it. The axle caught the shawl and twisted the child round throwing its head against the frame and sleeper. It was stated that the trolley was not the property of the Railway Company and had been loaned by a ganger named Rowland Edwards. Frederick Simms, a clerk in the employ of the Plinlimon *[sic]* and Hafan Company said the tramway was not yet opened for traffic. None of the men had permission to take any one of the trollies. A verdict of accidental death was returned'.

Official work's photograph of 1497, Treze de Maio, at the Castle Engine Works, Stafford.
Allan C. Baker

CHAPTER NINE

TALYBONT

In June 1896, W. G. Bagnall Ltd received an order from Collier Antunes* and Company for a locomotive of 2ft 5½in gauge (750mm) to work on a sugar plantation in Brazil, for which they were agents. She became works number 1497, a 2-4-0 side tank with outside frames, equalising beams and modified Baguley valve gear.¶ She was named *Treze de Maio*, which is Portuguese for the 'Thirteenth of May', the date of the legal abolition of slavery in Brazil in 1888. However, after she had been completed and photographed in February 1897, the order was cancelled and she was left on Bagnall's hands. There have been many fanciful reasons given for the cancellation, the most popular being civil war in Brazil. This is not the case as there was only a minor rebellion in the hinterland at the time, which was quickly put down. It is possible however that this affected the estates for which she was destined.

Then the Plynlimon and Hafan Company, who already had a locomotive on order from Bagnalls (to work the extension) approached them, looking for an engine at short notice to replace the ailing *Victoria*. 1497 fitted the bill, needing only a reduction in gauge, so Bagnalls quickly inserted spacing pieces on the axles, between the frames and the wheel faces, and dispatched her to Llanfihangel during mid-August 1897. She arrived, resplendent in a livery of black with a broad white line around the panelling, a thin red line inside that and the name *Talybont* painted on her side tanks. Whilst on the tramway she retained the spark arresting chimney, designed to prevent fires in the plantations, and a double skinned roof to deflect the heat of a tropical sun! During the winter months, she was fitted with a temporary sloping rear cab sheet. Two Talybont

* Boyd gives the name as Collier Antures, Cozens as Anturies and Davies as Antieres; the spelling I have used is taken from the Bagnall order book. Cozens also describes them as coal mine proprietors, but this is unlikely.

¶ Boyd gives Bagnall-Price valve gear but this was not patented until 1903, and reference to photographs shows that it was not fitted subsequently.

Talybont's dimensions were as follows:

Outside cylinders	8ft bore x 12in stroke
Driving wheels	2ft 2½in diameter
Pony wheels	1ft 4in diameter
Fixed wheelbase	5ft 0in
Total wheelbase	9ft 6in
Tank capacity	260 gallons
Bunker capacity	25 cubic feet
Heating surface (tubes)	160 square feet
Heating surface (total)	186 square feet
Grate area	5⅜ square feet
Working pressure	140 psi
Tractive effort (at 85% working pressure)	3,385lbs
Weight in working order	10 tons
Length	16ft 9in
Width	6ft 4in
Height	9ft 2¾in
Boiler length	6ft 9in
Boiler diameter	2ft 9½in

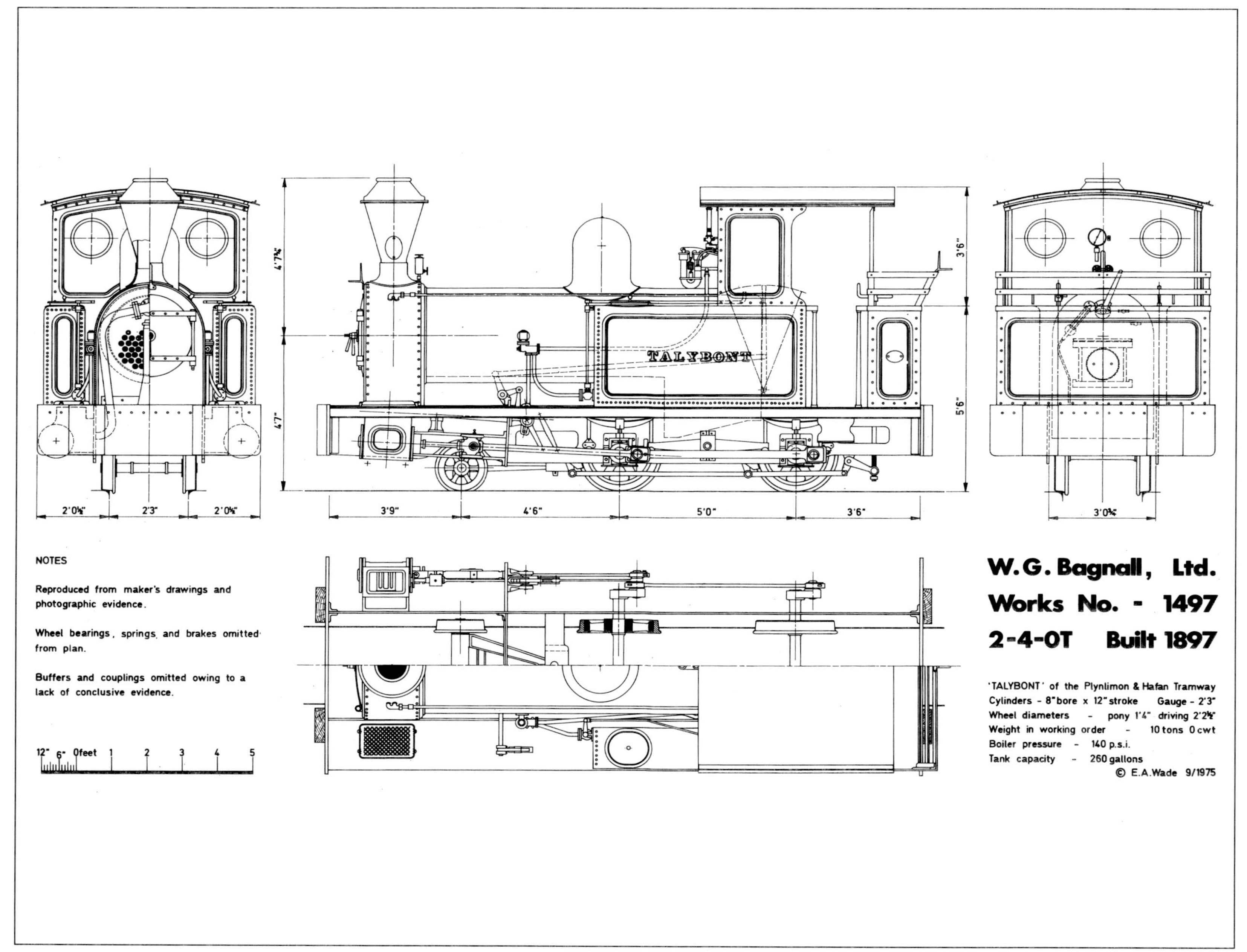
TALYBONT
4'7¾"
4'7"
3'6"
5'6"
2'0¾"
2'3"
2'0¾"
3'9"
4'6"
5'0"
3'6"
3'0¾"
NOTES
Reproduced from maker's drawings and photographic evidence.
Wheel bearings, springs, and brakes omitted from plan.
Buffers and couplings omitted owing to a lack of conclusive evidence.
12" 6" 0feet 1 2 3 4 5
W.G. Bagnall, Ltd.
Works No. - 1497
2-4-0T Built 1897
'TALYBONT' of the Plynlimon & Hafan Tramway
Cylinders - 8" bore x 12" stroke Gauge - 2'3"
Wheel diameters - pony 1'4" driving 2'2½"
Weight in working order - 10 tons 0 cwt
Boiler pressure - 140 p.s.i.
Tank capacity - 260 gallons
© E.A. Wade 9/1975

TALYBONT *and the remains of* VICTORIA *at Talybont station. Note the sloping rear cab sheet fitted to* TALYBONT *and the interesting items, to the right of the picture, which may have been removed from* VICTORIA. *The characters standing in front of* TALYBONT *are, presumably, her driver and fireman who also appear on the footplate in the photograph of the new* VICTORIA, *on page 33.* C. C. GREEN, FROM A COPY PRINT HELD BY W. E. HAYWARD

men, Evan Davies and David Jones, were her regular crew.

When the tramway closed, in 1899, *Talybont* was sold back to Bagnalls who in turn sold her, in July 1900, to Pethick Bros of Plymouth. Pethicks were the contractors for the Vale of Rheidol Light Railway, between Aberystwyth and Devil's Bridge, some ten miles to the south of Talybont. Thus, in 1901, Bagnalls re-gauged her yet again to the Rheidol gauge of 1ft 11½in and apparently modified the cylinders to 8in x 11½in. After working on the construction trains for two years, during which time a wooden cab back had replaced the sloping rear sheet, she passed into the stock of the Vale of Rheidol Company as their number 3, named *Rheidol*.

Before being put to work on this line, she was again returned to Bagnalls where a new firebox and vacuum brake apparatus were fitted in April 1903 and standard centre buffer-couplings in May, after which she returned to Aberystwyth, still bearing her balloon stack and wooden dumb buffers. Boyd states that she had disc pony wheels which were changed to spoked wheels when she was on the Rheidol. However, a glance at the maker's official photograph clearly shows that they had six spokes, as do photographs of her on the Plynlimon line. In an early photograph on the Rheidol she has discs, so they must have been fitted at her second re-gauging and later removed. A normal copper-capped chimney was fitted in 1904 and side chains replaced the dumb buffers. She was fitted with a steel cab back whilst the line was under the ownership of the Cambrian Railways. In 1923 the Great Western Railway assumed control of the line and she was allocated number 1198 (although she never actually carried it). She was finally withdrawn on 1 June 1923 and scrapped at Swindon on 17 July 1924.

1497 renamed RHEIDOL *in early days (c1902) on the Vale of Rheidol Railway. Apart from the change of name, she has been fitted with centre 'chopper' couplings, vacuum equipment, disc pony wheels and a wooden cab back.* C. C. GREEN

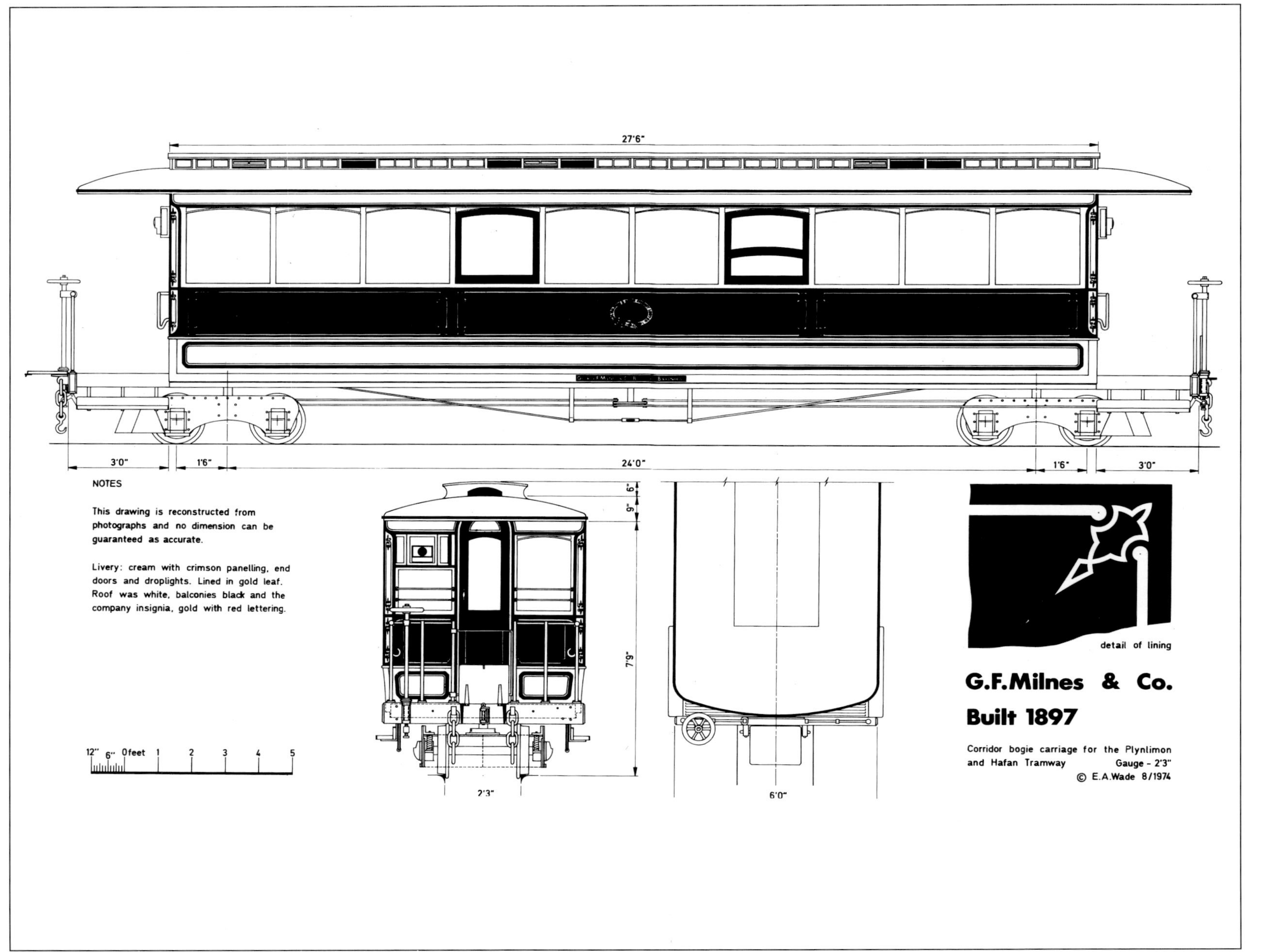

27'6"
3'0"
1'6"
24'0"
1'6"
3'0"
NOTES
This drawing is reconstructed from photographs and no dimension can be guaranteed as accurate.
Livery: cream with crimson panelling, end doors and droplights. Lined in gold leaf. Roof was white, balconies black and the company insignia, gold with red lettering.
12" 6" 0 feet 1 2 3 4 5
7'9"
9"
6"
2'3"
6'0"
detail of lining
G.F.Milnes & Co.
Built 1897
Corridor bogie carriage for the Plynlimon and Hafan Tramway
Gauge - 2'3"
© E.A.Wade 8/1974

CHAPTER TEN

CARRIAGE OF PASSENGERS

1897 – 1898

By the same train that brought *Talybont* to Llanfihangel came the tramway's only passenger vehicle. This was a bogie carriage constructed by Messrs George F. Milnes and Company of Cleveland Street, Birkenhead, who were, perhaps, the foremost tramway carriage builders of their day. They were, at this time, supplying vehicles (many of which are still in existence) to the tramways in the Isle of Man, notably the Manx Electric Railway. The Plynlimon carriage was very similar to these in its major details; even the lining appears to be identical. The Milnes Company dates back to 1860 when an American, George Starbuck, became the first tramcar builder in Britain, forming a limited company, based in Birkenhead, in 1872. George F. Milnes was Starbuck's secretary until 1886 when he bought the business from him. In association with German interests he opened a second, larger works at Hadley, Shropshire, in 1900, from where the whole business operated after 1902. The company went out of existence in 1904. However, in 1902 Milnes' son, George Comer Milnes, had started his own business in partnership with Thomas Voss, at the other end of Cleveland Street, Birkenhead. At first they only supplied tramcar accessories but later they built complete vehicles before closing in 1913.

The Plynlimon carriage was some 33ft 6in long over the beams, with bogies of 3ft wheelbase at 24ft centres. Molyneux tells us (in a letter dated 21 August 1897 to Mr P. P. Pryse) that it was designed to hold '36 to 40 according to size'. He was probably referring to the size of the passengers,

Maker's photograph of the carriage crossing the tram lines in Cleveland Steet, Birkenhead. J. S. WEBB

TALYBONT and the carriage on a special excursion at Bwlch-glâs. The mine is to the right of the picture but its overshot waterwheel can be seen beyond the engine. The photogrph fom which this drawing was produced, along ith those reproduced on pages 15 and 45, were clearly all taken on the same excursion: which is likely to have been that refered to on this and the following pages.
AUTHOR'S DRAWING FOM A PHOTOGAPH IN THE NARROW GAUGE RAILWAY MUSEUM

rather than the carriage. Access was by central sliding doors from balconies at each end of the coach and a corridor ran down the centre. The interior was divided into two portions by full height partitions which may have been fitted by the P&H, as they do not appear on the official maker's photograph.

Bench seats, probably of the slatted timber variety, ran along each side. The end balconies were fitted with screw handbrakes and wrought iron gates with let-down connecting platforms, which further suggests that the company had plans for increasing the passenger stock at some stage. The carriage ran on standard Milnes plate-frame bogies and was fitted with safety side chains; coupling was by a loose link. Oil lamps adorned each end and there was possibly some form of interior illumination below the clerestory lights. The livery was extremely intricate and must have looked well against the simple colours of the locomotives. The basic colour was cream, with crimson panelling, beading, end doors and droplights. The whole was lined out in gold leaf, which was particularly elaborate at the corners of the carriage. The bottom side panels were graced with a broad crimson line, with a thin gold leaf line inside. The company's garter device appeared in gold, with red lettering, centrally on each side. There were no class or running numbers but a long rectangular maker's plate appeared centrally, low down on the sides. The roof was white and the end balconies black.

On Thursday 19 August 1897, a trial run was made with *Talybont* and the carriage. They travelled from Talybont to the foot of the incline, both to test the engine and with a view to the commencement of regular passenger traffic. Some thirty people, including a number of women and children, availed themselves of a return ticket, and a large crowd greeted them on the train's return. Afterwards (27 August 1897) the *Cambrian News* had this to say

TALYBONT.

THE NEW RAILWAY. - There was great excitement at Talybont, last week, on the arrival of the new engine and passenger car for the Plynlymon *[sic]* and Hafan Railway, the new toy railway. The engine, which possesses all the modern improvements, has been proved to be thoroughly reliable and most suitable for the purpose. The car, which has been built on the corridor system, has most comfortable seats. It has also lofty headroom and its system of ventilation all tend to make the structure in every way perfect. There can be no doubt that it is due to the untiring energy and perseverance of the Managing Director (Mr Molyneux) that Talybont and district is in possession of such a serviceable and charming railway. A great boon has been conferred on the district by the provision of the railway which opens up means of communication with Llanfihangel Station and thence the main line. The toy railway will also be the means of bringing the varied and picturesque scenery lying between Talybont and Hafan more before the public. On Thursday afternoon a trial trip was made. Mr Molyneux was present, accompanied by Messrs Whitley, Stretton, Warrington, one of the directors, and Mr Councillor Shaw Green, Warrington, one of the shareholders. There were about thirty present to make the journey, amongst them being a fair sprinkling of ladies. After about half-a-dozen whistles a start was made. Naturally there was some excitement not unmixed with fear during the first few minutes, but the party soon gained confidence in their rather novel means of transportation. The varied scenery along the river Lerry was much admired, the sharp, rugged, and majestic mountains being a strong contrast to the grassy plots and green slopes. The party were taken past cots, through woods, along rivulets and streams. After accomplishing half the journey, a halt was made to quench the thirst of the little 'Puffer', which thoroughly deserved this slight refresher. A fresh start was made, and the party left with the good wishes and cheers of a few cottagers who had gathered to get a good view of the 'Train Bach'. The horses, cows, and sheep did not extend much welcome, as they rushed wildly in all directions. Possibly they were indignant at such an intrusion on their peaceful state. The party were now greeted with the sight of lofty mountains veiled in mist. A shepherd's boy could also be occasionally seen gazing open-mouthed in wonderment at what he probably considered the greatest marvel of the age. The 'Loco' soon after slowed and it was evident that the party were at their journey's end, nothing confronting them but a precipitous mountain. The party alighted and had a good view of the great incline they had ascended. After a short delay Mr Molyneux kindly undertook to act as guide and to show them round the Sett Stone Quarries. The scenery at the top of the steep path was simply glorious. On the one side were hills, valleys, and rapid brooks wending their course to the far-looming Cardigan Bay. On the other side stood Plynlymon like a giant over the lesser mountains, its crown being hidden from view by a steel grey mist. The party then proceeded to the Sett Stone Quarries of the Plynlymon and Hafan Co., Limited, whose headquarters are at 26, Castle-street, Liverpool. The object of the Company is to work the various industries in the neighbourhood of Talybont. Having arrived at the quarry, the party were amazed at finding such a large quantity of stone, the supply being practically unlimited. The beds are superficially situated, and can be worked with the utmost facility. The stones, which are of adamantine hardness, are trimmed and shaped into square setts for street paving. A flawless block of stone, weighing $7^1/_4$ tons, was forwarded to the Birmingham waterworks last week. A thorough inspection having been made, the excursionists retraced their steps towards the miniature train, and not in any way worried with the thought of having lost their return tickets. One whistle was now sufficient as there were no admiring spectators. On the return journey, numerous songs were sung, and a vote of thanks was passed to Mr Molyneux for providing the party with such a treat. 'Success to the railway' was also carried amid cheers. The train pulled up in the presence of a large number of the villagers who had assembled to welcome the safe arrival of the train. The railway will afford visitors to Aberystwyth an opportunity of investigating the comparatively unknown but truly beautiful scenery in the neighbourhood. Taliesin's Grave is within easy access of Talybont. The mining interests which have been dormant for a considerable period can now be revived if necessary, and then Talybont will once more resume its former position as a thriving mining village.'

Talybont and the carriage were a total success but the company felt that the track between Talybont and Llanfihangel was in need of some attention before passenger services could begin. It seems that the two previous accidents had, at last, instilled a sense of responsibility for public safety into the company. This may not be unconnected with the question of whether the tramway was entitled to carry passengers at all; it was certainly never authorised to do so by the Board of Trade. A passenger service began on Monday 28 March 1898, with the 9.20 a.m. from Talybont to connect with the Cambrian Railways market day special to Aberystwyth. The single fare between Talybont and Llanfihangel was 3d. and presumably there must have been another train to take the shoppers home in the evening. *The Cambrian News* commented...

'The opening of the narrow gauge railway from Llanfihangel to Tal-y-bont and Hafan for passenger traffic will make accessible for visitors staying in Aberystwyth a large extent of country interesting for its wild and romantic character...the engine, it appears, was built for a railway in Egypt...instead of running along the banks of the Nile and scaring the crocodiles, it is now climbing Welsh mountains and scaring Welsh sheep'.

Not a very accurate article for, as we have seen, *Talybont* was intended for Brazil. In addition, the passenger service only ran between Llanfihangel and Talybont on a regular basis, and never passed east of Pontbren-geifr except on special trains to the foot of the incline. The article also suggested that the passenger service would eventually climb the Hafan incline! It is possible that the carriage was augmented with wagons during the summer of 1898; the *Aberystwyth Observer* dated 7 April 1898 stated 'On Monday this railway was much better patronised by passengers'. As far as is known, passenger trains never ran on any other day of the week, with the exception of the special excursions to the foot of the incline, which proved very popular throughout the summer months. On these occasions light refreshments were provided, at the Hafan Mine, by Miss Grace Morgan of the White Lion, Talybont.

Despite these excursions the passenger service was losing money; there was little local demand for a service which only went two miles as it was almost as quick (and usually more convenient) to walk. Also, the time it took to raise steam in the engine was out of all proportion to the length of the journey. On 16 August 1898 Mr P. P. Pryse received a letter from Mr F. M. Simms stating 'At a meeting of the directors yesterday it was decided as the expense, etc, of running the car was so heavy the passenger traffic would be stopped, and consequently the

TALYBONT and the carriage again, just to the east of Bwlch-glâs Mine.
NATIONAL LIBRARY OF WALES

passenger service has been stopped until further notice'. It seems very unlikely that the service was ever resumed. Molyneux was visiting his brother in Tennessee, USA, when he heard the news. He was back in Britain in September. The carriage was eventually (presumably at the closure) taken to a garden at Llanbadarn (Aberystwyth) where it served for many years, stripped of its running gear, as a summer house. It is a mystery, considering how little use it had seen, why the company, or its makers, were unable to sell it to another railway; either in Britain or overseas.

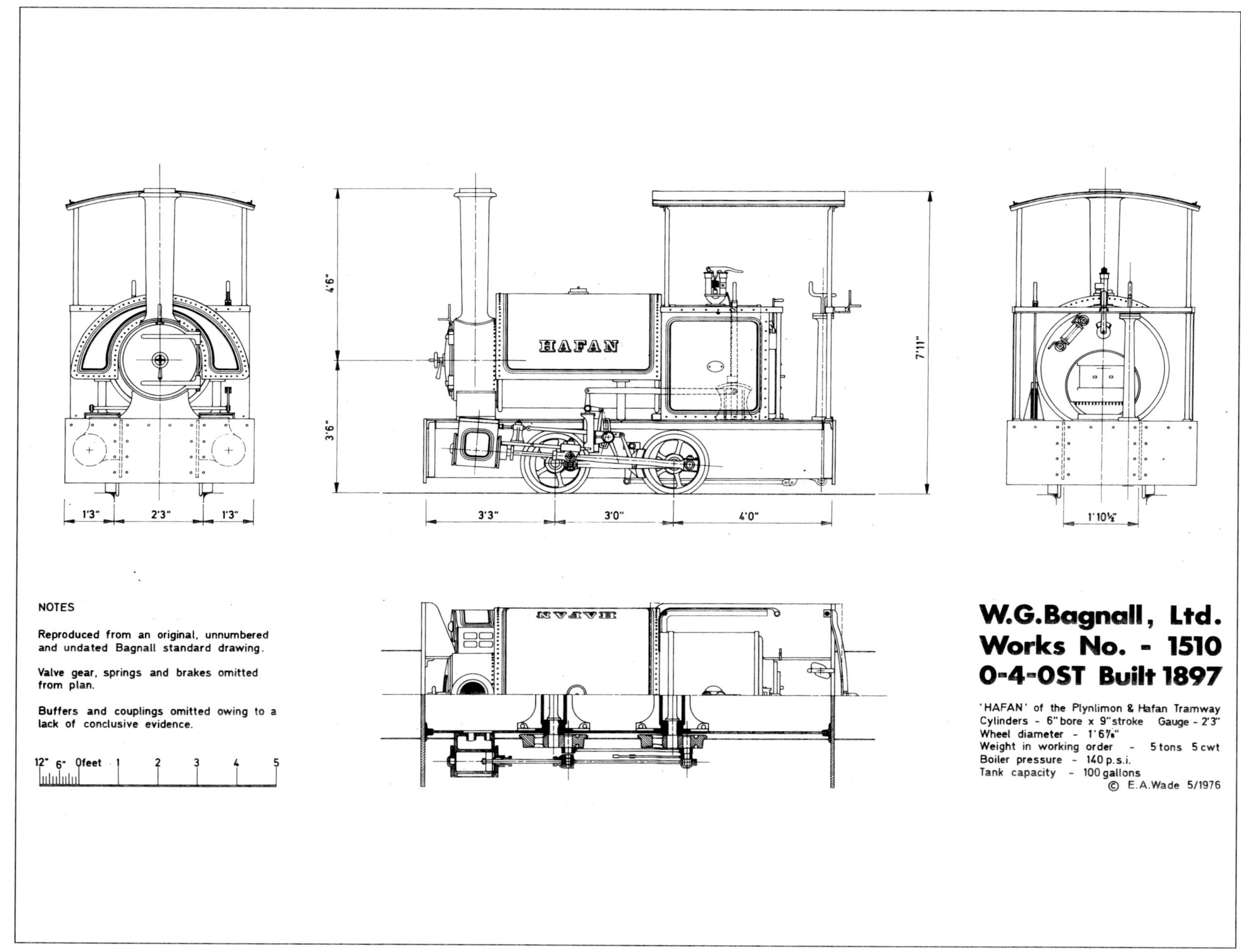
HAFAN
4'6"
3'6"
7'11"
1'3"
2'3"
1'3"
3'3"
3'0"
4'0"
1'10½"
NOTES
Reproduced from an original, unnumbered and undated Bagnall standard drawing.
Valve gear, springs and brakes omitted from plan.
Buffers and couplings omitted owing to a lack of conclusive evidence.
12" 6" 0 feet 1 2 3 4 5
W.G.Bagnall, Ltd.
Works No. - 1510
0-4-0ST Built 1897
'HAFAN' of the Plynlimon & Hafan Tramway
Cylinders - 6" bore x 9" stroke Gauge - 2'3"
Wheel diameter - 1' 6⅞"
Weight in working order - 5 tons 5 cwt
Boiler pressure - 140 p.s.i.
Tank capacity - 100 gallons
© E.A.Wade 5/1976

CHAPTER ELEVEN

HAFAN

The third and final engine to run on the tramway was Bagnall's number 1510; one of their small, standard, four-coupled saddle tank engines. She was one of a batch (1507-10) laid down for stock in March 1897 and was ordered by the Plynlimon and Hafan Company in the same month. She was delivered in September 1897, named *Hafan* and painted in the same style as *Talybont*. Fitted with Baguley valve gear, a cylindrical steel (marine type) firebox and steel tubes, she cost £336. During her time on the tramway, she worked exclusively on the extension, above the incline, and no photographs of her are known to exist. A photograph of her sister engine (1509) *Louise*, is included for reference. *Louise* worked on the Japanese Military Railways and is preserved (by the Japanese Railways) somewhere in that country. It should be noted that *Louise* differed from *Hafan* in having a full cab and sprung buffers.

When the tramway closed *Hafan* was hardly used and, in May 1901, Bagnalls re-purchased her. They sold her to Enoch Tempest for use on the Halifax Corporation's Walshaw Dene Reservoir contract. Before this sale the builders had to regauge her to three feet; not a difficult exercise as Bagnall's standard designs had many interchangeable parts, the only major new items being the frames and axles. She re-emerged bearing the name *Halifax*. By about 1910 she was in the possession of McDonald and Deacon, working on the Hurstwood reservoir in Burnley. In

Hafan's dimensions were as follows:

Outside cylinders	6in bore x 9in stroke
Driving wheels	1ft $6^7/_8$in diameter
Wheelbase	3ft 0in
Tank capacity	100 gallons
Bunker capacity	5 cubic feet
Heating surface (tubes)	80 square feet
Heating surface (total)	$89^3/_4$ square feet
Grate area	$3^1/_4$ square feet
Working pressure	140 psi
Tractive effort (at 85% working pressure)	2,043lbs
Weight in working order	5 tons 5cwt
Length	10ft 3in
Width	4ft 9in
Height	8ft 0in
Boiler length	4ft 3in
Boiler diameter	2ft $1^3/_8$in

Bagnall no. 1509, Louise, photographed in Japan.
ALLAN C. BAKER

about 1914 she was engaged on Keighley Corporation's Lower Laithe Reservoir, under the ownership of Messrs Morrison and Mason. New tyres were supplied at this time to Order No 1164, 24 November 1914. She later passed into the possession of the Bedley Timber Company of Nairn, Scotland. A new set of motion work was ordered for her on 11 September 1920 (Order No 4824) by one W. Reid* (presumably from Nairn). Boyd states that she was sold to the Beaulieu Timber Company in Hampshire, about 1925, after which all trace is lost. This may be the case but the author is worried by the similarity between Beaulieu Timber and Bedley Timber. She seems to have evaded the cameras in later life also and no Bagnall drawings of her are extant. However, there were so many engines of her type produced that it has been an easy task to re-construct a drawing.

* Cozens states that 1510 was 'ordered by Mr William Reid and was sold to Mr E. Tempest in 1897 for work on the extension'. Whilst it is possible that Enoch Tempest built the Hafan extension, the locomotive was certainly ordered by the Plynlimon and Hafan Company and the only reference to Reid in Bagnall's books is when he ordered the spares in 1920. One can only assume that Cozens was confused.

CHAPTER TWELVE

GOODS VEHICLES

Late in 1897 Bagnalls delivered some twenty-four mineral wagons to the tramway. These consisted of four stone wagons of eight tons capacity (nos 80 to 83), fifteen five ton stone wagons and five steel bodied coal tip wagons with a capacity of 62 cubic feet (nos 100 to 104)*. They were painted red, with 'P & H Co Ld' on the side, in white, with 'Talybont Cardiganshire' below. They all had screw brakes, hook couplers and pedestal axleboxes with single coil springs, and were well suited to the heavy mineral traffic which was expected on the line. The original Bagnall drawing of the four 8-ton stone wagons is still extant and carries the order number 444. The wagons had both end and side tipping doors and the standard Bagnall centre buffing/coupling gear should be noted. Their fate is not known.

The fifteen five ton stone wagons survived the closure of the tramway and, with *Talybont*, were bought by Pethick Bros, the contractors for the Vale of Rheidol Light Railway. Pethicks returned them to the makers to be regauged to 1ft 11½in and, on completion of the contract, they passed into the stock of the Vale of Rheidol Company, becoming VofR nos 1 to 15. During their time on this railway they have undergone many major modifications, which has led to a certain amount of confusion as to their original condition. They are said to have had end doors only and their bodies were probably 7ft 0in long by 5ft 4in wide by 3ft 0in deep. The wheelbase was 4ft 0in (somewhat short considering their capacity) and the wheel diameter 1ft 6in or 1ft 3in, otherwise the chassis was identical to the eight ton wagons. Three of the wagons were stripped and rebuilt as timber bolsters although one of them was more often seen without its bolster, running as a match truck. These conversions were the origin of a mistaken idea that only twelve P&H wagons ever ran on the Rheidol. Apart from these three body conversions it seems that the wagons remained in P&H condition until the Great Western Railway took over the Rheidol from the Cambrian Railways in 1923. They were considered very unstable by Swindon standards and so the chassis were completely rebuilt with a 5ft 6in wheelbase, standard GWR narrow gauge running gear and lever handbrakes. Re-timberings followed in 1938 and 1959 and seven still exist today under the private owners who purchased the line from British Rail. Four are locomotive coal wagons (now downgraded to four tons capacity) two are bolsters and one is the shorter of the two Rheidol flat wagons. Davies states that they had steel floors and safety chains in their original condition. This may be so, but if the eight ton wagon drawing is anything to go by, they were not fitted by the makers. Of the five steel bodied coal tip wagons no details are available but it seems likely that they were carried on a chassis of the same type as the other wagons.

The company is said to have also

* These numbers are given by Boyd and no reference to them has been found in Bagnall files. It is assumed that they are P&H running numbers but it is not known where Boyd got them from.

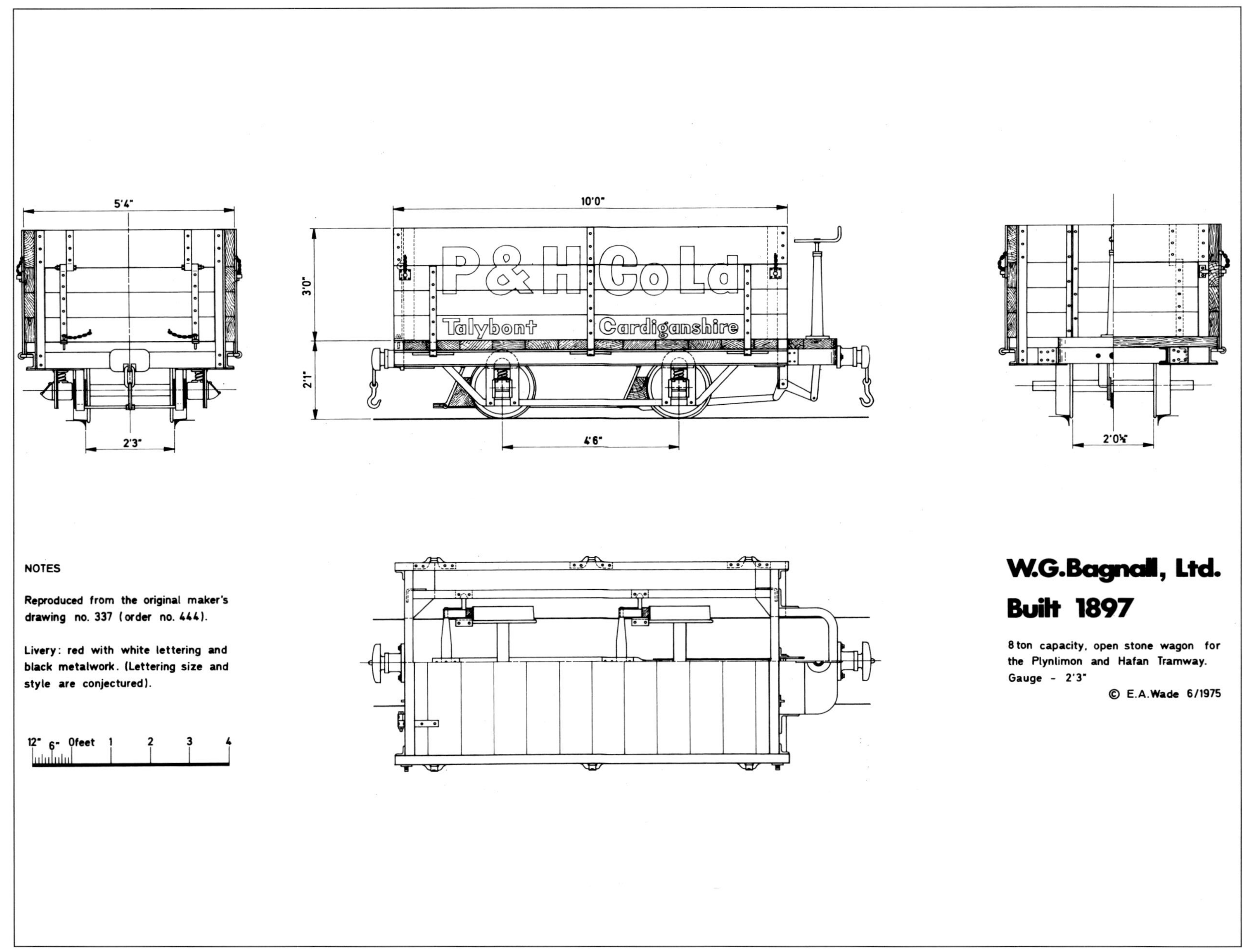
5'4"
2'3"
10'0"
3'0"
2'1"
4'6"
P&H Co Ld
Talybont
Cardiganshire
2'0¾"
NOTES
Reproduced from the original maker's drawing no. 337 (order no. 444).
Livery: red with white lettering and black metalwork. (Lettering size and style are conjectured).
12" 6" 0feet 1 2 3 4
W.G.Bagnall, Ltd.
Built 1897
8 ton capacity, open stone wagon for the Plynlimon and Hafan Tramway.
Gauge - 2'3"
© E.A.Wade 6/1975

owned a brake van and it is possible that this may have come from Bagnalls too. Looking at Boyd's running numbers (if that is what they are) for the wagons, there is a gap of sixteen numbers between 83 and 100 and if we take away the fifteen five ton wagons we are left with an odd number. This number may well have been allocated to the brake van, if we assume that all the vehicles were ordered together. It has been argued that there was no need for a brake van as all the Bagnall wagons (and the carriage) had their own screw brakes. However, a goods service is known to have commenced, with *Victoria*, in May 1897 (there was probably a horse drawn service prior to this) which indicates other, pre-Bagnall, wagons on the line (79 of them if the running numbers of the Bagnalls are anything to go by, but there may have been gaps in the list). The author has a theory that these included some type of flat wagon, used to transport stone slab and timber. This theory is based on two facts; firstly, the probable existence of a stone cutting shed at Llanfihangel and, secondly, the description of the vehicles involved in the two fatal accidents as 'trollies' or 'bogies'. These would be the obvious vehicles for the general public to ride on in the absence of a proper passenger service and it should be noted that, even after the arrival of the carriage, the passenger trains were very sparse. Thus, if people were determined to ride on these unbraked wagons, and in view of the two fatal accidents, it would be a logical step for the company to order a brake van. A letter from Molyneux to the estate (dated 29 May 1896) concerning the supply of timber gives exact details of trucks then being constructed. They had a body size of 6ft 5in long by 3ft 4in wide by 2ft 4in deep inside, constructed from planks 7in wide by 2in thick, and built to carry a load of four tons. It may be one such wagon that appears behind *Talybont* in the photograph on page 55. They would almost certainly have had

Model of 8 ton stone wagon.

Plynlimon and Hafan 5 ton stone wagon as rebuilt on the Vale of Rheidol.
E. A. WADE COLLECTION.

end doors and dumb buffers and the trollies would probably have been of the same length and width, with a timber bolster running crosswise in place of the sides. The company also possessed a velocipede, or manumotive trolley but no details of its construction have come to light. The rates charged by the company for the transport and delivery of stone from the top of the incline were as follows: to Cwmere 2s. per ton, to Talybont 2s.6d. per ton and to Llanfihangel 3s. per ton.

1497, now fitted with a conventional chimney, on a train at Devil's Bridge station, on the Vale of Rheidol Railway, in about 1907. This is the only photograph, known to the author, to show the ex Plynlimon and Hafan wagons on the Rheidol (albeit rather faintly) before they were extensively rebuilt. The end of one can be seen on the extreme left of the picture, coupled to another which has been cut down to make a match truck. Another, in original condition but for the regauging, can be seen just above the horse and in front of the timber bolsters; which are also ex P&H.
E. T. W. DENNIS & SONS POSTCARD.

CHAPTER THIRTEEN

CLOSURE

1898 – 1899

For a short time the tramway enjoyed some small measure of prosperity. Stone was sent to build the front at Aberystwyth, setts were produced for road construction and stone blocks were supplied to various industrial tramways, for use as sleepers. In 1897, the London County Council were considering a scheme for the construction of a waterworks in the Plynlimon area and such a project would, undoubtedly, have assisted the tramway. However, nothing materialised until, as we have seen, the Nant-y-môch Reservoir was constructed in the 1950s and 60s. Molyneux suggested to Mr P. P. Pryse, in a letter dated 24 August 1897, that further benefits would accrue to the line if a temporary branch were laid up to the ore house of the Bryn-yr-afr Mine. This branch would have been 2,600 yards long but, once again, nothing came of it. This was possibly because Mid Wales Mining Company, who owned the Bryn-yr-afr, were not prepared to pay the tariffs that the Plynlimon and Hafan Company wished to charge for the use of their line. By a special resolution, passed on 29 December 1897 and confirmed on 13 January 1898, the Plynlimon and Hafan Company increased their capital by the creation of 1,000 7% Cumulative Preference Shares of £10 each.

In April 1898, the Board commissioned T. Mellard Reade Esq, FGS, ARIBA, AMICE, to do a geological report on the area, from which we learn that...'The rock of Hafan Hill is principally a hard fine grained silicious and felspathic bluish coloured grit of Lower Silurian Age'. The setts proved to be of little use for the paving of streets as they were too hard and did not grit, and horses tended to slip on them. Also, the delivery of seven ton stones to the Birmingham Corporation's waterworks, in the Elan Valley, was stopped because the stone was found to have grain and it was liable to split under pressure. However, there is a story that the man who took the sample stones to Birmingham, for the crushing tests, was given financial incentives (by a company in Northumberland) to take completely different stones. The truth will probably never be known but it must be said that there are large farm buildings, built of Hafan stone, in the Leri valley, which appear to have stood up very well to eighty odd years of the Welsh climate and McAlpines were quite happy to use exactly the same stone for the new reservoir. Nevertheless, these problems, coupled with the steadily increasing costs of transhipment at Llanfihangel and Aberystwyth, and certain disagreements between the company and the Gogerddan Estate, rendered the quarry and tramway unprofitable and the whole system was closed down in the summer of 1899. Mr T. B. Steuart, the Managing Director of the Mid Wales Mining Company, wrote to the Plynlimon and Hafan Company, on 8 September 1899, seeking to reopen the tramway for the use of his own mines and to purchase the company's mines (except Bwlch-glâs) and the Hafan Quarry for some £5,000; but without any success. Had Mid Wales Mines shewn interest sooner, the fate of the tramway might have been very different. We learn from an

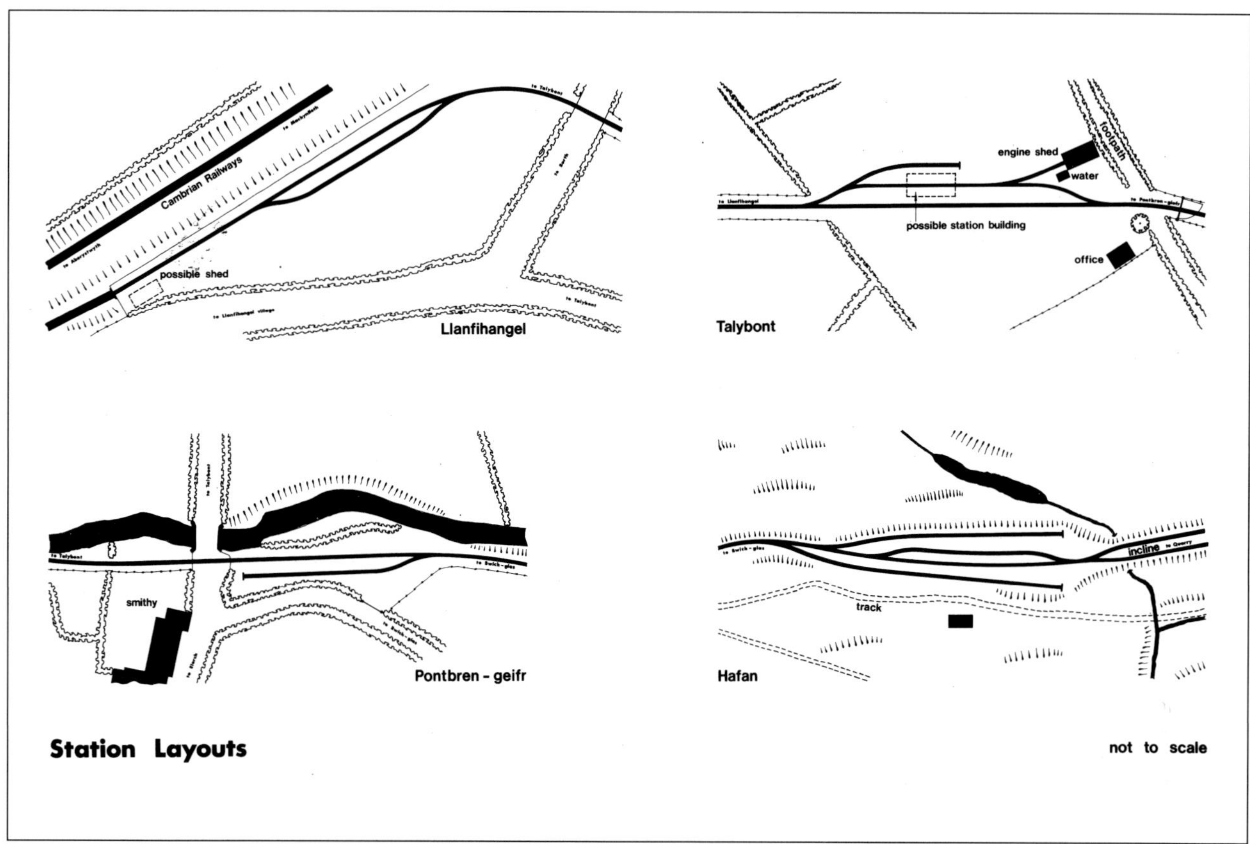

Station Layouts

indenture, reconveying land to Mr J. T. Morgan that,

> ...the Company on the Twentieth day of November One thousand eight hundred and ninety nine passed an Extraordinary Resolution to the effect that it had been proved to their satisfaction that the Company could not by reason of its liabilities continue its business and that it was advisable to wind up the same and accordingly that the Company should be wound up voluntarily and that the said Benjamin Cookson [presumably of Davidson, Cookson and Co.] should be the liquidator of the Company for the purposes of such winding up And whereas Notice of the said Resolution was published in the London Gazette on the Eighth day of December One thousand eight hundred and ninety nine....

The majority of the line was pulled up at the end of 1899 and its assets disposed of. Thomas Molyneux, Jnr, the General Manager and Engineer, returned to Lancashire where he died in 1946 but the fate of his father is not known. The company's timber office was taken to Glanfraed Farm for use as a hen coop and the office desk found a home in the corner of the same farm's dairy. Sir Pryse Pryse bought all the quarrying machinery with the exception of a few rock drills and the winding drum. The tramway was officially dead but it took many years to actually lie down.

CHAPTER FOURTEEN

CONCLUSION

1900 – 1914

The commencement of the new century brought the death, on 9 January 1900, of Mr P. P. Pryse at the age of forty. This closely followed the death of his father and the estate passed to the second son, Sir Edward John Webly-Parry Pryse, Bart. The 12 December 1902 edition of *The London Gazette* gave notification of a General Meeting of the company, to be held at 2 p.m. on Thursday 15 January 1903 at 6 Castle Street, Liverpool. The meeting was to inform shareholders of the way in which the company had been wound up. Notice of the dissolution of the company under Section 7(4) of the Companies Act, 1900, was finally given in *The London Gazette* of 19 March 1909.

Mr George Rice Pryse of Peithyll, Bow Street, Cardiganshire (the fifth son of Sir Pryse Pryse) now enters the scene with various new attempts at railway promotion in the area. During 1907 he was in communication with Mr Robert A. Smith, MIIE, a consulting engineer from London, with regard to an incredible proposal for the Great Western Railway to construct a standard gauge line. It was suggested that this should leave the GWR Dolgellau branch, just west of Bala Junction and proceed across, or through, the Berwyn Mountains to make an end on connection with the Mawddwy Railway at Dinas Mawddwy. The standard gauge Mawddwy

From about half a mile the incline looks almost vertical. TALYBONT and an unidentified wagon pass Allt-ddu farm, below the Allt-ddu escarpment. NATIONAL LIBRARY OF WALES

Railway, a length of 6 miles 63 chains, was opened in 1867 but was about to be closed to all traffic in 1908. It was reopened under the Cambrian Railways in 1911 and finally closed in 1951. From here the trains would have run over Cambrian metals to a point west of Glandyfi (or Glandovey) from where a new line was to be built through Tre'r-ddol, Tre-Taliesin and Talybont. The Cambrian line would be rejoined just to the north of Llanfihangel Station. It was suggested to the GWR that this scheme would give them a route to Aberystwyth from the north and enable them to link up with their line from South Wales. The tramway was to be relaid to connect the mines with the new system. The GWR however, had no interest in the project, which is hardly surprising as there is no way they could have made a profit out of building a line through the Berwyn Mountains. The response of the Cambrian Railways, if indeed they ever bothered to give one, is not recorded.

During the later half of 1909, Mr George R. Pryse entered into correspondence with Messrs W. A. and T. E. Thain, Consulting Engineers and Surveyors of Cardiff, who had clients who were interested in renting the Hafan Quarry and reopening the tramway to serve it. In the event the clients decided that the quarry was not financially viable and nothing came of the scheme.

The fourth attempt to reopen the tramway came in April 1910, when the aforementioned Robert A. Smith wrote to George R. Pryse on the 8th, quoting estimates for both narrow and standard gauges:

Proposed Mineral Line Llanfihangel to Hafan

NARROW GAUGE:	
Cost per mile	£1,106
Overall cost of Railway No 1	£3, 465
Overall cost of Railway No 2	£7, 224
Grand total overall cost of Railways 1 & 2	£10,689
New locomotive of 18 tons weight	about £800
or new locomotive of 22 tons weight	about £900
or second hand locomotive	from £400 - £600
Double bogie pressed steel 20 ton trucks with double hoppers, automatic couplings and centre buffers	from £200 - £250 each
Plain steel double bogie 30 ton trucks	about £180
Composite passenger carriage	about £500
STANDARD GAUGE:	
Cost per mile	£1,428.5s.
Overall cost of Railway No 1	£4,235.6s.
Overall cost of Railway No 2	£9,640
Grand total overall cost of Railways 1 & 2	£13,875.6s.
New locomotive	about £1,200
Second hand locomotive	from £500 - £700
No rolling stock to be bought.	

George R. Pryse contacted the Midland Railway Carriage and Wagon Co Ltd, of the Midland Works, Birmingham, to enquire into the cost of second hand 2ft 3in gauge 'fall down side' wagons. They replied on 15 March 1911 to inform him that they had no second hand wagons in stock, but enclosed a drawing and estimate for new wagons at '£32 each for not less than 12'.

Finally, in January and February 1914, Sir Edward Pryse was in correspondence with the Hafan Mining Co Ltd, the new owners of the Bryn-yr-afr Mine, who wanted to reopen the tramway for the use of that mine and the Hafan Quarry. The section from Llanfihangel to Talybont was to be built to standard gauge. A letter to Sir Edward Pryse from the Light Railway Commission, dated 9 February 1914, makes reference to a 'Proposed Llanfihangel and Hafan Quarry Light Railway'. The Hafan Mining Co Ltd was, however, in voluntary liquidation by June 1914 and, with the coming of the Great War, the lingering death of the Plynlimon and Hafan Tramway was brought to an abrupt end.

Since the closure, a great deal of information on the line and the company has been lost and the author is only too aware of the resultant gaps in this history; gaps which have been but little reduced in the twenty-one years since the first edition of this book appeared. With such incompleteness in mind, the author is content to have improved on what documentation has gone before and to have recorded, to the best of his ability, the history of a delightful, though short lived, narrow gauge tramway and the individuals who created it a century ago.

APPENDIX ONE

VICTORIAN REFLECTIONS

BY RODNEY WEAVER (1984)

(Reprinted from *The Narrow Gauge*, the Journal of the Narrow Gauge Railway Society)

Few British narrow gauge locomotives are more shrouded in mystery than *Victoria* of the Plynlimon & Hafan Tramway. So far as is known, it was its builder's one and only venture into the field of locomotives and if published accounts are correct it enjoyed one of the shortest careers of any British locomotive. The Plynlimon & Hafan itself had an active life of little more than two years, and the story of its rise and fall is well told in Ted Wade's history of the railway published in 1976, which includes both known photographs of *Victoria* and a reconstruction of the locomotive based upon same. Even this account leaves a few questions unanswered, however, and in the present article I shall attempt to provide answers to some of them. In doing so, doubt will be cast upon the assumption made by earlier writers that *Victoria* was a total failure and was laid aside as soon as the Bagnall 2-4-0 tank *Talybont* arrived.

Victoria was built by John Slee & Company of Earlestown, a firm of general engineers whose premises abutted the London & North Western Railway and appear in the background of several photographs taken here in the early part of the present century. The usual output of the works was marine auxiliary and stationary steam plant, pumps, etc., so it is not surprising that *Victoria*'s design embodied many features more appropriate to such machinery. Nor was it at all surprising that Slee should have built a locomotive for the P&H, for John Slee was a director of the Plynlimon & Hafan Company and Thomas Molyneux, the driving force behind the P&H, was a partner in John Slee & Co. Slee came into the P&H in a reorganisation brought about by its parlous financial state, so it would have been natural for him to offer his services in the construction of a locomotive for the railway at minimal cost.

Victoria was an enclosed, vertical boiler 0-4-0 not unlike a late model steam tram. It had an unusually long wheelbase, 6 feet, with outside flycranks and coupling rods. The boiler had an offset chimney in addition to what has until now been taken for a second one in the more conventional place at the top of the boiler. All accounts agree that it had four cylinders when new, two of which were removed when it became apparent that the boiler was too small, but as only two are immediately visible in the sole photograph known to show the locomotive as built there has been much speculation as to the location of the other two.

Taking the boiler first, the 'chimney' on top of the boiler is almost certainly a cowling round the safety valves. The chimney proper is that mounted on a smokebox protruding from the barrel just over halfway up the boiler. Clearly the boiler is an early version of the well-known Cochrane design, or a close copy of same, a type described at the time as 'vertical multitubular', which is not the clearest of descriptions. The Cochrane boiler was developed in Liverpool and manufactured in Birkenhead from 1877 until the firm moved to Annan in 1899. Slee may have purchased a Cochrane boiler for his locomotive, indeed he may have used them in his normal wares, or he may have made his own boiler in imitation of the early Cochrane type when the patents on this form expired. The significant point about Victoria's boiler is the shallowness of the smokebox compared with that fitted to later Cochrane boilers, a feature which suggests either a smaller number of tubes altogether or the use of a smaller number of larger tubes that was the practice in later years. Either way the boiler would be inferior to a 'definitive' Cochrane of similar size, and certainly unable to match the steaming capacity of a locomotive boiler of the same heating surface and grate area.

There is no mystery about the position of *Victoria's* second pair of cylinders. Close examination of a good print of the photograph taken at Talybont when the locomotive was new reveals a number of things that have apparently escaped earlier researchers. For a start, behind the coupling rod on the leading axle there is a marine-type big end attached to a connecting rod that disappears upwards into the superstructure. This is clearly the drive from the visible, vertical cylinder above the side sheet. Secondly, the bits and pieces in front of the smokebox resolve themselves into a sloping valve chest cover surmounted by at least one displacement lubricator. This is the missing pair of cylinders, inclined forwards at an angle of about 22½° and driving a cranked axle in the manner of a de Winton. That the valve chest is on the side of the inside cylinder block suggests the use of something other than Stephenson's valve gear and I suggest that Joy gear was fitted to obviate the need for eccentrics on the crank axle. The absence of eccentrics on the flycrank and the position of the valve chest on the vertical cylinder suggest to me that the valve of this cylinder is driven by a rocking lever from the inside valve spindle. If this were the case the inside and outside cranks could not have been diametrically opposite as in a conventional four-cylinder engine but would have been at something like 157½° so that the motions of the two pistons were complementary. If my deductions are at all correct the layout is surely too unusual to have developed by accident from the use of standard components, which suggests that Slee's decision to use four cylinders was a deliberate act.

This becomes more likely when one considers what was going on elsewhere in Britain at the time. 1897 was the year in which the four-cylinder simple expansion non-articulated locomotive made its appearance in this country, and it is just possible that *Victoria* was the first such locomotive to be completed. Being built at the same time at Crewe was F. W. Webb's first four-cylinder locomotive, *Jubilee*, which used simple expansion for comparison with the intended compound version. It is not generally realised that the divided-drive four-cylinder layout used by Churchward on the Great Western and by de Glehn in France was originated by Webb and included in his patent on multi-cylindered locomotives which covered the legendary three-cylinder compounds. When he came to build a four-cylinder machine of his own, however, Webb adopted single-axle drive because this gives total dynamic balance, unlike the divided drive method which is totally unbalanced in the vertical plane. Webb's locomotive used two sets of Joy gear to operate four sets of valves. John Slee must have been aware of what was going on at Crewe, and it is not impossible that he designed a four-cylinder locomotive in an attempt to overcome the inherent pitching motion which affects all vertical cylinder locomotives. With its cranks not set at 180°, *Victoria* would not have been as perfectly balanced as a conventional locomotive but would still have been much smoother in action than a two-cylindered machine. If Slee were influenced by Webb, it is a curious coincidence that Webb's locomotive also had inadequate boiler power for the total cylinder volume used.

Victoria was delivered to the P&H on 12 May 1897 and was soon found to fall well short of its builder's expectations. Within a couple of months the P&H were looking for a replacement and found one waiting for them in Bagnall's works. *Talybont* arrived at the beginning of August and it is generally assumed that this marked the end of *Victoria's* brief career. I feel it more likely that she lasted a bit longer and was not finally discarded until August 1898 when the passenger service was terminated. Her poor performance is easily explained: the boiler was too small. Slee being unfamiliar with locomotive practice perhaps had recourse to a textbook and failed to realise that a square foot of heating or grate surface in a locomotive boiler is worth two or three in any other form of boiler. The leading dimensions of *Victoria* and *Talybont* were probably similar, but the latter's boiler had a much higher output. A Cochrane boiler of similar size to that in *Victoria* was reckoned to be capable of steaming continuously a twin-cylinder winch with 6in cylinders. *Victoria* had four cylinders of this size.

My own calculations suggest that *Victoria* had 20in wheels, not 18in as suggested by Ted Wade, and that it had 6in x 10in cylinders. Assuming a boiler pressure of 120psig, its nominal tractive effort would have been 3,600lb, which is in keeping with a service weight that cannot have exceeded seven tons. By comparison, *Talybont* had a nominal tractive effort of 3,200lb at 80% boiler pressure. Neither locomotive would have been a particularly mindblowing performer on the upper part of the Plynlimon & Hafan where the ruling gradient was 1 in 19. One cannot but observe that the P&H was a singularly bad railway. If a gradient of 1 in 19 could not be avoided, and I am not convinced that it could not have been, then the line should have been engineered to a standard that permitted the use of locomotives large enough to haul a reasonable load. Instead it was laid with 30lb/yd flat-bottomed rail, almost the lightest track to be used on any Welsh mineral line, and *Talybont* was about the largest locomotive that could safely have run over the line. Had traffic grown to the proportions once envisaged by its promoters the limitations of this cheap track would have become embarrassingly obvious!

Assuming that the locomotives were worked at 80% of their theoretical maximum capacity, the loads that they could have hauled over the entire length of the line were as follows:

Victoria in four cylinder form	15 tons
Victoria as reduced to two cylinders	4 tons
Talybont	10 tons

Victoria's apparent advantage in original condition would have been dependant upon being able to produce enough steam, which it could not, and upon good adhesion. The latter could not have been guaranteed in the average Welsh winter! When reduced to two cylinders it was of no use whatsoever on mineral traffic, hence the advent of *Talybont* as soon as the fatal defect in her make-up was recognised.

A two-cylinder *Victoria* could, however, have been used quite successfully on passenger trains which did not normally run beyond the 'station' of Pontbren-geifr. The ruling gradient to this point was only 1 in 33, up which *Victoria* could have handled a load of 12 tons in two-cylinder form. That would have been enough to haul two fully loaded coaches of the type purchased by the P&H, and given that the solitary coach actually bought was seldom full during the short career of the P&H passenger service *Victoria* might well have been more appropriate, and probably more economical, motive power than the larger *Talybont*. It seems quite possible that *Victoria* was tried out with two cylinders disconnected, in which form she would have proved rather lively due to the lack of balance, and that having proved reasonably successful in this form she was taken out of traffic for more extensive modification. This would entail removal of the redundant cylinders, requartering of the crank axle and the addition of balance weights, an operation which would mean setting the locomotive up on blocks to take out the axles. It is in just this position that *Victoria* appears in the photograph showing both locomotives at Talybont at an unspecified date.

Whenever it has appeared in print hitherto, this photograph has been described as showing the 'discarded' *Victoria*; but there is no justification for this assumption. For one thing, one does not start an expensive rebuilding operation on a locomotive that has already been written off. More telling is the lack of a date for the photograph. If it were taken in late 1897 or early 1898 it may show *Victoria* under active reconstruction as suggested in the previous paragraph, in which case she may have returned to traffic in time to haul a few passenger trains before these were abandoned in August 1898. On the other hand, if it were taken later than mid-1898 then it may show *Victoria* in a state of suspended animation, rebuilding having been abandoned with the decision to end passenger services. Useful though she would have been on these lighter duties, once they ceased the railway could have had little use for a locomotive that was not an adequate deputy to *Talybont* on mineral workings. August 1897 may not have been the end of *Victoria's* short career but August 1898 almost certainly was, and in retrospect it was also the beginning of the end for the Plynlimon & Hafan itself.

If *Victoria* was far from being the most successful narrow gauge locomotive to run on a Welsh railway she was surely one of the most interesting. The use of four simple cylinders in a non-articulated locomotive was a singularly advanced idea for its day and the locomotive may have been the first of its type to run in Britain. The use of Joy valve gear was unusual in a British narrow gauge application, too, though far from being unique even in Wales. There were at least two de Wintons fitted with this gear, probably for the same reason that it would have been used in *Victoria*, and from photographs of these it is possible to imagine what the invisible parts of *Victoria's* mechanism may have looked like. One was Pen yr Orsedd's *Arthur*, built in 1895, on which Joy gear was clearly an original fitting. The other was the locomotive belonging to the Moel y Gest Quarry in Portmadoc, the subject of a well-known photograph showing it in Harbour Station around the turn of the century. This locomotive had apparently been rebuilt by the Falcon Engine & Car Works and it is possible that the engine with Joy gear shown in the photograph was not the original. That raises the interesting question of its origin, for one school of local thought has it that *Victoria* ended her days in North Wales...

COMMENTS BY E.A.WADE (1984)

In his article on *Victoria* of the Plynlimon and Hafan Tramway... Rodney Weaver states that he will 'attempt to provide answers' to unanswered questions. He provides only attractive but unsubstantiated theories, without supporting evidence.

Since writing my book on the P&H, some eight years ago, I have done some further research; particularly into John Slee and Thomas Molyneux. Molyneux was, indeed, a partner in John Slee & Co. but had made his money from a grocery, furnishing and drapery business which was established in Earlestown in 1853. This business expanded steadily, as did the town, and, by 1895, Molyneux was also the proprietor of a bakers, a boot and shoe dealers and a wheelwrights. However, following his disastrous investment at Hafan, the business contracted again but still occupied 37-41 Market Street (at least) until the Great War. John Slee was a neighbour of Molyneux's, living at Moss House, Wargrave, Earlestown. The date of the founding of the Earlestown Engineering Works is unknown to me but, by 1881, 'John Slee & Co., Engineers and Millwrights' was established there according to the local directory. Slee disappeared from these premises some time between 1897 and 1901; presumably bankrupt. Rodney tells us that the Earlestown Works 'abutted the London & North Western Railway' but the directories give the address as Cross Lane; two streets from which there is, incidentally, a Foundry Street. I do not know where Rodney got the idea that John Slee & Company's 'usual output' included marine steam engines. I have before me a sheet of their notepaper, dated June 1896 (i.e. at about the height of Slee's success and when he must have been commencing work on *Victoria*) which gives a list of their products as follows: 'makers of horizontal and vertical steam pumps (single, double and quadruple-acting), pumping engines, duplex pumps, gas compressing engines, winding engines, air compressing engines, hauling engines, blowing engines, 'Slee's' friction clutch, and underground haulage machinery. Iron and brass founders'.

The fact that Slee advertised his ability to manufacture 'quadruple-acting steam pumps' would seem to reinforce the tradition that *Victoria* had four cylinders. She may well have done and Rodney's speculations as to their position seem quite reasonable; but the hard evidence of two photographs only prove the existence of two cylinders. The same comments apply to Rodney's surmise as to the layout of the boiler. He tells us that *Victoria* performed poorly because 'the boiler was too small' (by which he means too small for the demand placed upon it) and that she 'had four cylinders' which he calculates to have been 6in bore x 10in stroke. He also states that 'when reduced to two cylinders it was of no use whatsoever on mineral traffic'. Now let us assume that the cylinder size he gives is correct and that two were removed (or never fitted). De Wintons were built with two 6in x 10in or even 6in x 12in cylinders and a boiler about 5ft high by 2ft 9in diameter. *Victoria's* boiler was more that 5ft high and with a diameter (which can be measured from photographic evidence) of 4ft. The extra size and weight of *Victoria* over a de Winton could, no doubt, counteract the larger boiler size; so why should not *Victoria* have steamed just as well as a de Winton?

Rodney goes on to tell us what loads *Victoria* and *Talybont* were capable of hauling up the ruling gradient of 1 in 19 (actually 1 in 18.3) on the upper section of the tramway. He totally misses the fact that all the goods traffic went down the line and could have been worked by gravity. The only up traffic was empty wagons and men. The passenger service, which normally ran between Talybont and Llanfihangel (not to Pontbren-geifr as suggested by Rodney) twice a week, certainly could have been handled by *Victoria* considering the gentle gradients on this section. It could also have been pulled by *Talybont* which was likely to have been in steam for other purposes anyway. In short, the traffic did not justify two locomotives in steam.

The other photograph of *Victoria*, to which Rodney refers, could indeed show her in a partially rebuilt condition, but it is probably more accurate to describe her as 'out of use'; anything else is pure conjecture. Finally, I consider it inconsistent to state: 'John Slee must have been aware of what was going on at Crewe' and, in the next paragraph, continue: 'Slee being unfamiliar with locomotive practice'.

Reply by Rodney Weaver (1984)

I made no claims that I would leave no unanswered, possibly new questions because I know very well that a lot of historical research proceeds by moving from one set of questions to another.

As to the alleged inconsistency in

suggesting that John Slee knew what was going on at Crewe but was ignorant of the fundamentals of locomotive design, I fail to see what Ted is complaining of. Slee's works was close to the LNWR's principal wagon works, happenings at Crewe were reported in the technical press, Slee was himself a mechanical engineer: it seems highly likely that he knew in basic terms what was afoot. Moreover, as a builder of steam engines he would appreciate the advantages of a balanced four-cylinder layout. On the other hand, he did not design and manufacture his own boilers (had he done so then Ted's letterhead would surely have proclaimed the fact), and thus is unlikely to have appreciated the basics of proportioning a boiler to its intended duty in an application very different from those to which his normal products were applied. He might have looked in a builder's catalogue, noted the grate area and heating surface of a locomotive about the same size as *Victoria* and ordered a boiler from his normal supplier accordingly. It seems possible to me, and it was only put forward as a suggestion. There are several precedents for mistakes of this kind, for instance Brunel's specifications for the original GWR locomotives.

Victoria's boiler I now believe to have been of the Nicholson Patent variety. This was a variation on the basic Cochrane theme and enjoyed a degree of popularity in the 1890s for steam cranes and similar intermittent duties. It had a side-mounted rectangular smokebox surmounted by a short, wide chimney almost exactly as on *Victoria*. To compare this boiler size-for-size with a de Winton one is misleading because the two boilers were of totally different design. The Nicholson was a true stationary boiler, designed for a moderate average steaming rate but capable of sustaining short periods of heavy demand. The other was a vertical multitubular boiler capable of a higher sustained output in relation to its grate area, a true vertical locomotive boiler in fact. For this reason I feel that Ted's comparison is invalid: size-for-size a de Winton boiler would have been able to feed four cylinders against the Nicholson's two, so it isn't really surprising that a much smaller de Winton boiler sufficed for two 6in x 12in cylinders.

Ted's description of the P&H rolling stock omitted the tare weights of the vehicles. (Ted's source was primarily the original working drawing, which gave no weights. Ed.) I find this to be a common failing in railway histories generally, yet the tare weight of a vehicle is one of the most important statistics from an operational point of view, and in the case of the P&H it is my reason for doubting the usefulness of either locomotive had any significant level of traffic been established. The P&H wagons were engineered to a standard that should really have been applied to the track, the wagon now on the VofR having a tare weight of two tons for a capacity of five tons (four tonnes on the VofR). By contrast, a Festiniog wagon of similar capacity weighed 28cwt, little more than two-thirds as much. Reducing my estimated load to empty wagons, we get the following working loads over the upper section of the line:

Victoria as built	8 wagons
Victoria two cylinder	2 wagons
Talybont	5 wagons

True, loaded trains could run by gravity, but before a loaded wagon could come down an empty one had to go up, and if one looks at it in that light one round trip by the rebuilt *Victoria* yielded a mere eight tons of downward traffic. Even *Talybont* would handle only twenty tons per round trip. That is under ideal conditions. A single loaded wagon going up to the mines would reduce the load by three empty wagons! It is on this basis that I suggested for the rebuilt *Victoria* the role of passenger locomotive, for had traffic increased significantly *Talybont* would have been fully employed keeping the mines supplied with empty wagons. As Ted rightly says, that situation never arose, but the P&H were not to know that at the time.

One final point. Ted says that I gave Slee's manufactures as including marine steam engines. I did not. I used the term auxiliary which embraces pumps, winches, etc. but excludes the main propulsive machinery. Perhaps it was an overstatement to suggest that marine work was an important aspect of his business, but I would be surprised if a fair number of his pumps and winches did not find their way into locally-built ships.

FURTHER COMMENTS BY E.A.WADE (1985)

I am amazed that Rodney Weaver should have based his suppositions about the carrying capacity of the Plynlimon & Hafan Tramway on the wagons now at Aberystwyth. To the best of my knowledge no drawing or photograph of these wagons in their original 5 ton condition survives. There is a maker's drawing of the larger, 8 ton version which I redrew for my book and the two types are believed to have been similar except for some 3 feet difference in length.

All fifteen 5 ton wagons were bought by Pethick Bros, converted to 1ft 11½in gauge and used on the construction of the VofR; later becoming VofR 1 to 15. When the GWR took over in 1923 they totally rebuilt these wagons. The wheelbase was increased from 4ft to 5ft 6in, standard GWR running gear and side lever brakes were fitted in place of the original pillar brakes, and the channel solebars appear to have been replaced by a larger section. The timber bodies were repaired or replaced in 1938, 1959 and 1980-81. At some stage they were also downgraded to 4 tons capacity.

Thus, the wagons now on the VofR bear no relation to the originals and are, almost certainly, considerably heavier. This simple fact makes Rodney's calculations somewhat suspect.

A FINAL NOTE FROM BRIAN BENNETT (1986)

The photograph of Slee's works mentioned by Rodney Weaver...appears in *The London & North Western Railway* by C. C. Dorman (Priory Press Ltd, 1975). It shows 'John Slee and Co., Engineering Works' in large block capital letters on the gable end of the building, and the picture seems to have been taken from platform four of Earlestown station, the platform for trains from Warrington. If this is so, then the works would have been situated in Old Wargrave Road.

APPENDIX TWO
PRINTED MATTER

HOUSEHOLD STORES,

37, 39 AND 41,

MARKET Street,

EARLESTOWN.

PURE MALT EXTRACT DIGESTIVE BREAD.

Having taken up Montgomeries Patent for this, a trial is respectfully solicited, This Extract is not only used for the malt Digestive Bread, but is also used in all our Bread and Cakes, thus ensuring to the public the very best and most nutritious Bread and Cakes.

SOLE LICENSED BAKER FOR THE DISTRICT.

DEPARTMENTS:

GROCERIES:

TEAS, COFFEES, FLOUR, BAKING, CORN, PROVENDER, PROVISIONS.

FURNISHING:

BEDSTEADS, FURNITURE, BEDDING, HARDWARE.

DRAPERY:

GENERAL.

ALL GOODS OF THE FINEST QUALITY.

T. MOLYNEUX,

PROPRIETOR.

BUSINESS ESTABLISHED, 1853.

Advertisement from The Newton and Earlestown Guardian (8 July 1898) for Thomas Molyneaux's Household Stores.

PLYNLIMON AND HAFAN COMPANY, LIMITED.

J.W. DAVIDSON, COOKSON & Co.
CHARTERED ACCOUNTANTS.
TELEGRAPHIC ADDRESS.
"DANTON, LIVERPOOL".
TELEPHONE No. 545.

48, Castle Street,
Liverpool, 15th march 1897

Plynlimon & Hafan Company headed notepaper - actual size

TELEGRAPHIC ADDRESS:
"SLEE'S EARLESTOWN."

MAKERS OF
HORIZONTAL AND VERTICAL
STEAM PUMPS
(Single, Double, and Quadruple-acting).
PUMPING ENGINES. DUPLEX PUMPS.
GAS COMPRESSING ENGINES.
WINDING ENGINES. AIR COMPRESSING ENGINES.
HAULING ENGINES. BLOWING ENGINES.
"SLEE'S" FRICTION CLUTCH, AND
UNDERGROUND HAULAGE MACHINERY.
IRON AND BRASS FOUNDERS.

JOHN SLEE & Co.,
EARLESTOWN ENGINEERING WORKS,
EARLESTOWN,
LANCASHIRE.

June 8th 1896.

John Slee and Company headed notepaper - actual size

APPENDIX THREE
LOCAL RAILWAY RELICS

In the first edition of this book an appendix was included which discussed the possible origins of four railway vehicles, two carriages and two vans, which stood (and hopefully still stand) on the cliffs above Borth and saw service as a holiday cottage. Measured drawings of these vehicles were also included and it was thought that they might have some connection with the Plynlimon and Hafan Tramway. However, subsequent research by Robert Nicholls has shown that no such connection existed and the interested reader is directed to *Manchester's Narrow Gauge Railways* by Robert Nicholls (Narrow Gauge Railway Society, 1985) where the present author's drawings are reproduced.

Molyneux's lead mines at Esgair-hîr and Esgair-fraith were connected by a two feet gauge tramway of some five furlongs in length, built of bridge and inverted T section rail, laid in chairs. This was almost certainly horse worked and boasted an incline and various bridges. A detailed history of these two mines (although not covering the period when they were worked by Molyneux) was produced by Marilyn Palmer in 1983 and is referred to in the bibliography.

At Camdwr-bâch there was a line of unknown gauge, about ¾ mile in length, connecting a distant level with the main mine.

(Left) The author poses in Ty-nant cutting, 1976. P. Holman

(Right) 1996. E. Davies

APPENDIX FOUR
THE 1896 PAMPHLET

'A brief description of the Plynlimon and Hafan Narrow Guage 2ft. 3in. Tramline and the district it traverses and will serve'

The present terminus is at Llanfihangel, six miles north of Aberystwith, on the Cambrian Railway. The little line practically follows the trend of the river Leri as far as Cwmere, at this point it crosses and leaves the Leri, and follows the trend of the Maesmawr Stream, a tributary of the Leri. The line commences in the east at Carn Owen, locally named Hafan, it may, however, be ultimately extended to Mount Plynlimon, and even beyond, for it is probable that the Great Dyliffe Lode, part of which was worked by Cobden and Bright, will be re-started, as I understand very good lead has again been discovered.

In passing, I wish to remark that some people have a floating idea that all the lead in Wales has been worked out, and against such an idea I protest most strongly, and, without the slightest hesitation, I affirm that there is vastly more yet than has ever been got out of Wales. At the present moment my friends and self are working at a newly discovered deposit ranging from 4 in. to 24 in. thick solid lead, and that only in adits, but besides that, most of the deposits are only worked in shallow depths.

To resume; the line at present is only laid to Carn Owen, but I wish to describe the district a little east of this. At Great Dyliffe and Huddgen very good Lead exists. Coming westward, to Drosgol, there exists a deposit of low grade Ochre, interspersed with dark red patches of earthy matter, which may prove to be useful for terra cotta or the like, besides the red patches of earthy stuff, nuggets of Manganese suitable for a dye are interspersed, the whole being in the form of segments of an arch. Where this Ochre and Manganese, &c., came from is a question; the Nuggets are more like the slag from a furnace than anything else I can think of. Dr. Harries, of Aberystwith, informs me that there is a little silver in them. That gentleman, and another Aberystwith gentleman, hold the place from the Woods and Forests Commissioners. *

It has been stated that the only known deposit similar is Broken Hill in Australia, and if that is so, it is certainly rare enough to be very interesting indeed. The last time I was round there there stood up, between Drosgol and Plynlimon, a very nice lump of Conglomerate; I presume it is there still.

Coming westward still, we arrive at Camdwr Mawr, where fine Lead is being mined by some Glasgow and Edinburgh gentlemen, and the last time I was there, a few weeks ago, they had come across a new find, a specimen of which was at the office, and splendid it was, and being encrusted with bright pyrites was a beautiful sight.

Across their boundary we enter on the first section that is being worked by my friends, and the first place being worked is on the same lode as the last named workers, and the same indications have come in as encountered by them at starting, viz:—Pyrites and Blend (Zinc Ore). About 600 yards westward, we have found Copper Ore as well as Lead, and now we come to the great beds of Stone, which have been the cause of the little line being made. All who have visited this immense body of Stone have been surprised and astonished, and when it is stated that at an output of 3,000 tons a week there is ample and more for 3,000 years, the surprise and astonishment become enhanced. Some term it Trap Rock, others Syenite, but I think if it is termed Silurian Grit it will be correct.

At a point about 1½ miles north from here there is a nice bit of Contorted rock well worth seeing by those sufficiently interested.

To keep, however, to the route of the line we find here at these beds of hard grits the perfect curvature, and truly it is wonderful, from north to south, a length of over a mile, with the curvature east and west of a base of over 500 yards. It would appear as though, at a point about ¼ of a mile from its southern extremity, this huge mass has been cloven in twain by the mineral lode which now passes across and through it. Lying against the western side of these hard grit beds we find the dense slaty Silurian beds, and overlying these again the shales. Three quarters of a mile west again we come to Llechwdd Helig, where the shales were cut by forming the bed for the line, and where, at two points, small ribs of lead were cut. Half a mile west again we arrive at the place where we are obtaining such fine lead. This occurs in the compact dense slaty Silurian, and right opposite, to the north about 200 yards, in the bed of the stream, the strata of rock, slaty Silurian, is perpendicular, so that from here to the foot of Carn Owen, the Anticlinal must have succeeded the Synclinal, and it is probable we shall find some traces of the change.

A mile westward again we come to what I can make into nothing else than a glacier grooved rock, and respecting which I want more able opinions. Another mile west, and we again arrive at perpendicular slate beds. Half a mile westward again we arrive at what has evidently been a lake, several layers of various kinds having been exposed in making the bed for the line, sand, clay, gravel, and conglomerate, and about 200 yards further on, either a continuation of this, or a similar, but smaller one. The old river banks show that at some period the river was of a good size, and many feet higher than it now is.

Westward again, about 500 yards, we come to a deposit of fine blue clay, evidently the grindings by the glaciers of the blue Silurian, ground so fine that the paste is quite smooth and sticky. At two places in this part we find fine sand.

We now arrive at Talybont, two and a quarter miles from Llanfihangel. Where Talybont now stands there has evidently been, in former times, a large lake, or it may have been a large hollow in the sea bottom. The indications are that the river formerly flowed out at the north-west end, but eventually found its way out at the south-west end. In several of the small cuttings from here to Llanfihangel small sections were encountered of conglomerate in embryo, almost as hard as concrete ; in fact, blasting had to be resorted to. In Glonfraed cutting, shales were met with, interspersed with blocks of the dense slaty Silurian rock. At Llanfihangel, on excavating for the siding, a deposit of finely ground shales was the result, which has proved very useful for ballast, being porous, yet very even. This would appear to be the grindings by the glaciers of the shales overlying the dense slate, and the fine blue clay the grindings by the glaciers of the dense slate rocks. For so short a line, about 7½ miles, the variety of deposits is very great, and carrying as it does, the imagination back to the ice age, makes it very interesting. For, in imagination, we can picture Carn Owen stone overlain by the dense slaty Silurian, this again overlain by the shales, then the commencement of the ice age, then the slow thaw, and the slow moving of the ice mass, crushing, grinding, pounding, irresistibly moving and carrying along enormous masses of rock, for we find one mass close to Talybont, about 7 tons weight, 5 miles from its origin, and other masses of Carn Owen stone all along the valley. And there is no mistaking it ; there is no other like it.

Of the very best kind for paving setts, macadam, ashlar work, and local building, it is sure to command a very large sale, and at the moment I am writing I have an enquiry for all we can make for the next few months. Speaking of the district, I have arrived at the same conclusion as the late Sir Warrington Smythe, that it is the most prolific metaliferous district in Cardiganshire. See Book II, Part II, Geological Survey of Great Britain.

* At a point about 3 miles south-west from Drosgol, but not on the route of the line, there is a deposit of finely ground Manganese, mixed with earthy matter, the Manganese, 60 % of the mass, evidently being the nuggets ground by the Ice Masses, and if so, proves it to be heavier than the red earthy mineral, which at that spot lies above the ground Manganese as a layer, not intermixed.

After the Geological visit at Easter a more thorough description will be written, accompanied by a tracing of present line and proposed extensions, east end and west end, traced on a Geological map, which in turn will show the mineral lodes* of the district in fine gold lines, also the new lode, so called, because only discovered within the last 5 years, and found to carry Lead and Zinc Ores, and Pyrites.

SOURCES & ACKNOWLEDGEMENTS

In the production of this volume I have been given invaluable assistance by many people, especially local residents, which I cannot properly acknowledge as I neglected, in many cases, to record their names. However, special thanks are due to Allan C. Baker for his seemingly endless supply of information on W. G. Bagnall and Company, to Simon Hughes and his family for supplying me with a bed and victuals on my visits to Talybont, besides much information on the mines of the district, to Keith Pearson for information concerning G. F. Milnes and Co, to D. H. Cozens (brother of the late Lewis Cozens) for permission to reproduce information and photographs from his brother's booklet, to the staff of the National Library of Wales, to Don Boreham, the late Mr T. O. Jones (Talybont), Mr Paul Abell and to Dave Newson for reading the manuscript. A final thank you is due to Messrs S. King and P. Holman for digging up more information as I was about to go to print.

In the years which have passed since the first edition of this book appeared, little additional information has come my way, but I cannot let this opportunity pass without thanking C. C. Green for his notes on the layout of the junction between the P&H and the Cambrian and copies of cuttings; Brian Malaws and D. J. Percival, for the latter's very detailed sketch maps of the whole of the trackbed, drawn a year or two before I first visited it, and for photographs of the Coed-y-cwm bridge; and to Rodney Weaver for his thought provoking speculations about the Slee locomotive.

BIBLIOGRAPHY

The principal source of reference for this work has been *The Gogerddan Family Papers* in the National Library of Wales, which contains much of the estate correspondence for the period of the tramway's construction and operation. Sadly this consists, mainly, of incoming letters only and one is left to speculate about what the replies may have been.

Anon. *A Brief Description of the Plynlimon and Hafan Narrow Guage 2ft 3in Tramline and the District it Traverses and will Serve* 1896

Baker, A. C. & Civil, T. D. A. *Bagnalls of Stafford* Oakwood Press 1973

Bick, David E. *Old Metal Mines of Mid Wales, Part 3 Cardiganshire - North of Goginan* Pound House 1976

Boyd, J. I. C. *Narrow Gauge Railways in Mid Wales* Oakwood Press 1952, Second Edition 1970

Bradley, V. J. & Hindley, P. *Industrial and Independent Locomotives and Railways of North Wales* Birmingham Locomotive Club, Industrial Locomotive Information Section 1968

Christiansen, Rex & Miller, R. W. *The Cambrian Railways Volume 2* David & Charles 1968

Cozens, Lewis *The Plynlimon & Hafan Tramway* Author 1955

Davies, W. J. K. *Vale of Rheidol Light Railway* Ian Allan 1970

Green, C. C. *The Vale of Rheidol Light Railway* Wild Swan Publications 1986

Hughes, Simon J. S. *Cardiganshire - Its Mines and Miners* Author 1976

Kidner, R. W. *The Cambrian Railways* Oakwood Press 1973

Lewis, W. J. *Cardiganshire Historical Atlas* Cymdeithas Lyfrau Caredigion Gyf 1969

Palmer, Marilyn *The Richest in All Wales, The Welsh Potosi or Esgair Hir and Esgair Fraith Lead and Copper Mines of Cardiganshire* Northern Mine Research Society 1983

ARTICLES:

Anon. 'Vale of Rheidol Wagons Restored' *The Narrow Gauge* No 92 1981

Baker, Allan C. 'Jessies, Concords & Polar Bear' *The Narrow Gauge* No 84 1979

Baker, Allan C. 'Margarets & Mercedes' *The Narrow Gauge* No 89 1980

Baker, Allan C. 'Rheidol: Putting the Record Straight' *The Narrow Gauge* No 132 & No 133 1991

Boyd, J. I. C. *The Railway World*, January 1954

Leleux, S. A. *The Railway Modeller* February 1969

Pascal, R. A. (letter) *Stephenson Locomotive Society Journal*, November 1952

Weaver, Rodney 'Victorian Reflections' *The Narrow Gauge* No 102 1984, and subsequently in Nos 104, 108 and 112.

NEWSPAPERS:

The Aberystwyth Observer
The Cambrian News
The Welsh Gazette

INDEX